DATE DUE

DISCARDED

GAYLORD			PRINTED IN U.S.A.

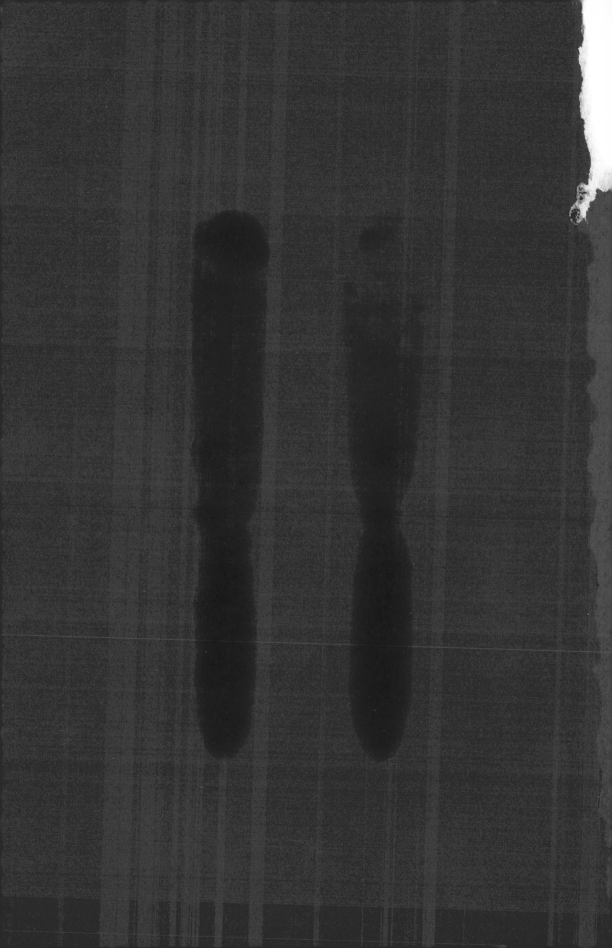

BEAUTIFUL LEAVED PLANTS

BEAUTIFUL LEAVED PLANTS

FRANCES PERRY, MBE, FLS, VMH

with a note on Benjamin Fawcett by

Ray Desmond

DAVID R. GODINE
Publisher - Boston

First published in the United States in 1980 by
DAVID R. GODINE, PUBLISHER, INC.
306 Dartmouth Street
Boston, Massachusetts 02116

ISBN 0–85967–316–8
LCC 79 90555

Printed in Great Britain

Contents

Introduction

The beauty of leaves, with their infinite variety of shape and coloring, has fascinated artists, sculptors, and plant lovers over the centuries. Plants with bicolored and even tricolored foliage, or with beautifully fringed or delicately cut leaves, perhaps with intricate veinings, are not only a delight in themselves but also make splendid companions for flowering plants.

In the second half of the last century foliage plants were extremely popular. The grand drawing rooms of Victorian houses all had their quota of palms and ferns, but in those houses heated by coal fires the plants had to put up with extremes of temperatures. The atmosphere would be overheated during the day and fall close to freezing at night, and few plants relish such conditions. Thus the conservatory became an almost obligatory adjunct to the house of a well-to-do Victorian family. Many a proposal of marriage was made to a blushing damsel among the palms and ferns in the conservatory.

In these structures, where the temperature and humidity could be more effectively controlled than in the house, a wide range of plants could be grown. Some of them would be taken into the house to do a turn before being brought back to the conservatory to convalesce. But shortage of fuel and labor during the 1914–18 war and the ever increasing costs of both in the period between the wars spelt the end of the Victorian conservatory, and interest in foliage plants waned considerably.

The color plates in this book are taken from two Victorian books, *Beautiful Leaved Plants* (1861), by E. J. Lowe, and *New and Rare Beautiful-leaved Plants* (1870), by Shirley Hibberd, published in the heyday of the fashion for indoor plants. I have drawn on Lowe and Hibberd in writing my text, and Ray Desmond writes about the plates, and the remarkable wood engraver who printed them, at the end of this book.

PLACING YOUR PLANTS

Since the 1950s there has been a tremendous revival of interest in foliage plants. Central heating in houses and apartments has made it possible to grow numerous pot plants successfully, although with many plants it is often difficult to maintain a degree of humidity that will satisfy them. Picture windows, sun lounges, and garden rooms built on to houses have provided even more happy quarters for foliage plants. As a result, millions of these plants are propagated and sold every year. Old varieties have been rediscovered, new varieties and even new species have been brought into cultivation, and there is a wide choice of plants that will grow in almost any surroundings. Some, such as scindapsus, *Saxifraga stolonifera*, cissus, and *Begonia rex*, will support living-room conditions permanently.

But there are many more that can be brought into the house for some weeks and then, as they begin to show signs of disliking their lodgings, they can be returned to a greenhouse. In recent years thousands of small greenhouses have been built in amateurs' gardens, and many of these are used in part to grow foliage plants that may be brought into the home for a time or even for a special occasion. In a greenhouse with glass to the ground, many foliage plants grow very happily under a bench.

Observant gardeners will have noticed that house plants often do better in communities than when grown singly, an arrangement that also provides pleasing effects in the home. The plants may be grouped in a variety of ways, but since a moist atmosphere is essential for many plants, the humidity aspect should be considered. Plunging the pots in a large container, such as a copper preserving pan, and packing them around with moist peat – kept constantly damp – is one method. Or they may be stood on gravel trays, which can be bought from garden shops and come in various sizes. Over the bottom of these spread an inch of washed gravel, granite chips, long-fiber sphagnum moss, or such synthetic materials as clay granules or expanded shale, and pour a little water in the base. When the pots are stood inside they will feel the influence of the moisture beneath without actually standing in it.

In this book, of course, there are plants, such as the ivies, that are perfectly hardy and may be grown in the open or in pots indoors. The hostas are hardy too, as are aucubas and lily of the valley. Some plants need winter protection under glass but may be placed outside for the summer months, while others in temperate climates must spend their lives under cover.

Most of the plants illustrated in this book are available from florists or specialist growers, but some of the rarer and very beautiful varieties may survive only in botanic gardens and private collections. It is to be hoped that publication of this book may elicit information about the whereabouts of some of these older but very desirable varieties. And some of the species described, no longer cultivated, may still survive in their native lands.

In general, the hardy foliage plants described will grow in the open and enjoy any reasonably fertile, well-drained soil, and the varieties are tolerant of sun or partial shade. Those with variegated, golden, or silver foliage, however, give of their best in full sun, tending to become more green with less light. This applies also to variegated plants grown indoors, although it may be necessary to move some species out of direct sunlight during the hottest months of the year.

Some plants, such as the hostas, dislike a situation where they are subject to the drip of rain from overhanging trees, and although they revel in shady or mainly shady positions, they should not be planted directly under trees. Ivies, on the other hand, do not object to dense shade and indeed are excellent plants to grow as ground cover under trees. As the tree leaves fall they should be brushed with a twig broom so that they will lie below the ivy foliage, there to rot down and eventually fertilize the ivy.

SOIL MIXES AND FEEDS

The majority of the plants illustrated, however, are grown in pots or other containers. The old gardeners used to have their own jealously guarded secret recipes of soil mixes for the different plants; even the under gardeners were banished from the potting shed while the head gardener prepared his special mixes. These magical formulae included cow or sheep dung, loam, or leaf mold, so old and rotted that it was as light as sphagnum moss, with a dash of soot or lime, ingredients once easily found in gardens on large estates but now for most of us, alas, hard to come by.

Apart from specific mixes for individual plants, reference is occasionally made in this book to John Innes Seed and Potting Composts. The formulae for these composts were devised by the John Innes Research Institute, now based at Norwich, England, in the 1930s. They were carefully planned so as to provide a basic soil mixture for a broad range of plants. They are widely used by growers as well as amateurs in Britain, but virtually unknown elsewhere in Europe and in the United States. Both in Europe and the United States, however, there are plenty of commercial prepackaged potting and seed mixes, which can safely be substituted for John Innes.

John Innes Seed Compost is made up as follows:

2 parts, by loose bulk, medium, partially sterilized loam

1 part, by loose bulk, peat

1 part, by loose bulk, coarse sand

To every bushel of the above mix add $1\frac{1}{2}$oz superphosphate and $\frac{3}{4}$oz ground limestone or chalk.

John Innes Potting Compost is composed of:

7 parts, by loose bulk, partially sterilized loam

3 parts, by loose bulk, peat

2 parts, by loose bulk, coarse sand

To every bushel of the above mixture add $1\frac{1}{2}$oz superphosphate, $1\frac{1}{2}$oz hoof and horn ($\frac{1}{8}$in grist), $\frac{3}{4}$oz sulphate of potash, and $\frac{3}{4}$oz ground limestone or chalk. Certain plants, especially those that make a great deal of growth in a year, often require a stronger mix. Accordingly, the chemical compound (known as J. I. Base) is doubled, to make John Innes No. 2 Potting Compost and trebled for No. 3 Compost. Once the chemicals are added to the base ingredients they start to break down and change, so it is important to use the material as fresh as possible.

We may make up our own mixes of loam, peat or leaf mold, and sand for cuttings or for potting, if we can find the loam, but good loam is becoming scarcer every year. In recent years commercial loamless mixes based on peat or bark fiber have gradually taken over from the loam-based mixes, and for most plants these have proved eminently satisfactory. Peat-based mixes are more difficult to wet again if they are allowed to dry out. If this happens, the best method is to stand the pot almost up to its rim in a bucket of water and allow the water to rise by capillary action until the ball of mix is wet again. Alternatively, one can water the pot, leave it for half an hour, and water it again. Some gardeners add coarse, well-washed sand to their peat-based mixes to give added weight to the pot, as large plants tend to be top-heavy in pots filled only with a peat mix. Peat mixes should have the advantage of being free from weed seeds and disease spores.

The great house-plant firm of Thomas Rochford of Hoddesdon, England, has also devised formulae for certain plants. Thus for aroids they recommend 2 parts loam, $1\frac{1}{2}$ parts leaf mold, 1 part sharp sand, and $\frac{3}{4}$ parts rotted farmyard manure – all parts by bulk – adding a 5-inch flowerpot full of superphosphate to every barrowload of the mixture. For begonias they use 2 parts each of loam and peat, $1\frac{1}{2}$ parts leaf mold, and 1 part sand.

Further information on these and other growing points can be found in T. Rochford and R. Gorer's excellent book *The Rochford Book of House Plants* (Faber) [or, in the United States, *The Treasury of Houseplants*, by Rob Herwig and Margot Schubert (Macmillan)].

For seed sowing, fine mixes are used, but coarser mixes are normal for potting or repotting. With peat-based mixes it is important that they should *not* be firmed down when one is preparing a seed box or when potting or repotting plants. They should merely be watered well after sowing or potting to consolidate the mix. If they are firmed with the fingers as one does with the old loam-based mixes, the plants may become waterlogged and losses may occur.

Nowadays plastic pots are rapidly taking the place of clay pots, and though most plants grow as well or even better in plastic, more care is needed in watering when plastic pots are used. With clay pots water evaporates through the sides, so the plants need watering more frequently than do those in plastic pots.

When potting plants, make quite sure that there is free drainage at the bottom of each container, otherwise the roots will become waterlogged and die. Plastic pots usually have several drainage holes and therefore need only a thin layer of roughage over their bases. Dry leaves, coarse peat, or sphagnum can be used for this purpose. Clay pots with only one hole should have this hole kept open by the placement of a few pieces of broken clay flowerpot in the base and then a thin layer of roughage.

Healthy indoor plants normally require feeding during the growing season. There are many house-plant fertilizers on the market, most of them based on nitrogen, potash, and phosphate. Use these as directed by the makers – never at greater strength, or you may kill your plants.

Some commercial fertilizers work through the leaves. These are called foliar feeds and are applied in water by being sprayed over the foliage.

Also, never apply a liquid fertilizer to a plant if the soil is dry, as it may damage the roots. Water the plants first and then apply the dose of fertilizer. Many growers find that it often pays to apply a fertilizer twice as often as recommended by the manufacturer, but at half-strength. This system works particularly well with pelargoniums and begonias. Feeding should be given only when the plants are in active growth in spring and summer, and should be withheld in late autumn and winter, when most plants are fairly dormant.

Mulching provides another form of feeding, particularly for outdoor plants. This involves spreading a layer of organic matter, such as decayed animal manure or garden compost, moist peat, or leaf mold, on the soil around the plants. As this rots down the salts released feed the plants. The material also keeps the roots cool in hot, dry weather.

PROPAGATION

Propagation of the plants illustrated may be effected by seed, cuttings, air layering, or by division of the roots; indication of the appropriate method is given in the descriptions that follow. Seed sowing is very simple. Large seeds are just covered with the seed-sowing mix, while very small seeds may be sown on the surface of the mix and covered with the merest sprinkling of fine silver sand. The pot or seed box is then stood in water until the mix has drawn up enough water to saturate it. Then a sheet of glass is put over it and this is turned over every day. To prevent the pot or box from drying out unduly, cover it with brown paper until the seeds germinate. There is a popular misconception that seeds will germinate only in the dark, but with the exception of one or two genera all seeds will germinate in full light.

Many plants are easily propagated by cuttings. Of the plants described in this book soft cuttings, i.e., young shoots produced earlier in the year, are the best. Much depends on the condition of the young growth. If the shoot is too soft it may rot. If it is left too long and has become semi-woody it may root but it will take a long time to do so. One has to learn by trial and error the correct stage of growth for taking the cuttings.

Usually a cutting is made from a young shoot two or three inches long, the cut being made just below a node or leaf joint. The lowest pair of leaves is removed. In the case of pelargoniums there is a tiny green whisker at the point where the leaf joins the stem. This must be removed, as otherwise it will rot and cause the death of the cutting. Always use a very sharp knife or a razor blade when making cuttings, since if the base of the cutting is bruised it will probably rot. With many plants it is helpful to dip the base of the cuttings into one of the hormone rooting compounds containing a fungicide such as captan. This not only hastens rooting but also reduces the risk of the cutting's being affected by some soil-borne disease.

According to the quantity involved, the cuttings are then inserted in pans, pots, or seed trays of sandy soil. Set them firmly and then water them with a watering can with a rose at the end. Place them in a warm propagating frame to root, or stand them in a deep box with 3 inches of moist peat over the base, setting this in turn over a warm radiator. In summer they will usually root without such need for bottom heat, for example on a kitchen windowsill. A sheet of glass or plastic sheeting should be placed over the top to maintain humidity and to keep the cuttings from wilting; this should be removed for half an hour daily to change the air and prevent water droplets from falling on the plants. Whilst rooting, the cuttings should be protected from the sun.

Some plants, such as peperomias and begonias, may be propagated by leaf cuttings. One method is with a razor blade to make cuts across, but not through, the main veins under the leaf and then to lay the leaf on the surface of a pot filled with sand. The leaf is kept in close contact with the moist sand by being pegged down with a hairpin or two, or weighted with a couple of pebbles.

Another method of rooting leaf cuttings is to cut the leaf into several segments, leaving a section of a main vein in each, and inserting them with the vein vertical in the rooting mix. By the first method young plants can be produced at the points where the veins are cut, and by the second method young plants may appear at the base of the cutting.

With all cuttings it is desirable to maintain a soil temperature of 18–21C (65–70F) and a steady high humidity. This is easy if one has an electrically heated propagating case, but a small number of cuttings can be rooted quite simply if they are put in a pot or box filled with a suitable mix – say, half peat, half coarse sand – and then covered with a tightly fitting transparent plastic bag. Of course, it may be necessary to put in a few short sticks to keep the plastic from touching the plants, because if this does happen, condensed moisture may run down the plastic onto the cuttings and cause rot to start. If the pots or boxes are kept in a warm greenhouse or on the windowsill of a warm room, excellent results may be expected.

Some plants, such as cordylines and yuccas, may be propagated by air layering. This is a very simple yet effective method of reproduction, and is used when the plant grows too tall for its quarters in the living room or greenhouse. At a convenient point, where there is a leafless area below the crown of the plant and beneath a node or joint, remove a narrow strip of bark, a quarter-inch wide, all round the stem. Don't go beyond the green cambium layer into the heartwood. Next dust the cut with a hormone rooting powder and then pack damp sphagnum moss over the whole area – around the cut and an inch on each side. Secure it lightly with damp raffia and then wrap clear plastic film over the whole, securing it at top and bottom with adhesive tape. The result will be a sausage-shaped package. Eventually roots will grow from the cut, and when these are seen through the film, separate the new plant from the old one and pot it up.

Propagation by division is very simple, and plants such as lily of the valley and hostas may be increased in this way. The plants are best lifted and divided in autumn or spring. Only strong young growths from the outside of the plants should be used to transplant and form new plants.

PESTS AND DISEASES

Pests and diseases are not normally a big problem with foliage plants. Molds and mildews, however, will affect some plants, especially if they are growing in a damp and stagnant atmosphere. Plants in a greenhouse or in the home should be inspected every day or two. Decaying or withering leaves should be removed. At the first sign of disease (usually moldy spots on the leaves) the plants should be sprayed with a suitable fungicide. So too with pests – aphis (green- or blackfly) and whitefly, caterpillars, red spider mites, scale insects, thrips, or mealy bugs. One should look for signs of damage, such as mottled, twisted, or weakened shoots or foliage. There are many insecticides available nowadays to control these pests. But to be really effective they must be applied as soon as the infestation is noticed, and repeated as quickly and as often as advised by the manufacturers.

Well-cared-for plants, well fed and watered regularly, will usually ward off diseases and be less affected by pests than poor or neglected specimens. Good husbandry has always paid good dividends.

A NOTE ON PLANT NAMES

In the descriptions facing each plate I very often give the name of the natural order to which the plant belongs (*natural order* is an older synonym for *family*, and is used in place of it throughout the book). The natural order is given in Latin, and appears in roman type, e.g., Malvaceae. The name of the genus, or subdivision within the natural order, is given in italics, e.g., *Abutilon*. A genus is divided into species, and this is shown by another Latin name after that of the genus, e.g., *Abutilon megapotamicum*. Where there is a cultivated (i.e., not a naturally occurring) variety, its name is given, after the names of genus and species, in roman type with quotation marks, e.g., *Caladium bicolor* 'Chantinii,' where *Caladium* is the genus, *bicolor* the species, and 'Chantinii' the name of the variety introduced by and named after M. Chantin in 1857; for a variety not named after a person, var., in roman type, and the name, in italics, follow the genus and species (e.g., *Calathea rotundifolia* var. *fasciata*). A multiplication sign, as in Musa × *paradisiaca*, indicates the crossbreeding of two species. The specific name at the top of each section of text refers to the illustration opposite; often the text that follows is of a more general nature.

Plates

(The plates are numbered 1–64,
and this numbering is used for cross-references
in the facing text.)

Abutilon striatum 'Thompsonii'

RED-VEIN ABUTILON

Abutilons are shrubby evergreen plants belonging to the natural order Malvaceae. *Abutilon striatum* comes from Brazil, where it makes a shrub or small tree with slender shoots clothed with very thin, toothed, three- or five-lobed green leaves. The variety 'Thompsonii' was introduced by Veitch and Son in 1868 from a plant found in the West Indies. It is still widely grown, especially by parks authorities for summer bedding purposes, in greenhouse work and for floral displays. But it also does very well in pots in sun lounges and bright hallways, the normal height being 1–1.5m (3–5ft). The long-stemmed leaves are smaller than those of the species and richly mottled in yellow and dark green – colours which contrast pleasingly with the salmon-pink, red-veined, pendulous flowers.

Plants bloom when quite small, even from cuttings taken the same season, and flowering continues right through autumn if conditions are warm enough (10c, 50f minimum). Abutilons need plenty of light at all times and should be grown in a rich potting compost like John Innes No. 3 Potting Compost or a mixture of equal parts (by bulk) of turfy loam, peat, leafmould and sharp sand. Good drainage is essential so all containers should be well crocked. The plants will need plenty of water during the growing season and occasional feeds with a liquid fertilizer during the summer.

The plants are easily increased from cuttings taken in spring or late summer. These should be rooted in a sand and peat mixture in a warm propagating case (18c, 65f), but after potting they need cooler conditions (15c, 60f or slightly over). Keep them on the dry side in winter and prune back old plants in spring before restarting them into growth.

A few abutilons have economic uses. The crushed leaves of *A. trisulcatum* are reputed to be a specific against mouth cancer; *A. graveolens* is cultivated in Russia for the seeds which produce an edible oil; and the fibre of several others is used for cordage and various coarse fabrics.

Acalypha wilkesiana Hybrid

COPPER LEAF

Acalypha wilkesiana, also known as *A. tricolor* or more popularly as copper leaf, comes from the New Hebrides and belongs to the natural order Euphorbiaceae. In tropical gardens it makes a large bushy shrub, 2–3m (6–10ft) tall or larger, but in cool, temperate climates it is usually grown in pots and rarely exceeds 30–60cm (1–2ft). Another common name, 'match-me-if-you-can', refers to the tremendous variations in leaf colouring, no two leaves being patterned exactly alike.

Many varieties of *Acalypha wilkesiana* have been named, but the species is so variable that these are constantly being superseded and the old ones lost to cultivation. Basically, however, the nettle-shaped leaves are ovate with toothed margins, and blotched, mottled or splashed with red and crimson on a coppery-tinted green background. The flowers are insignificant.

For pot culture grow the plants in a rich compost like John Innes No.2 Compost or a made-up mixture composed of equal parts by bulk of coarse sand, sifted loam and moist peat or leafmould. Greenhouse specimens should be frequently sprayed with soft water to ward off white fly attack – a troublesome pest with acalyphas. Aim at growing temperatures around 15–18c (60–65F) or more; but not below 10c (50F), and feed weekly.

Propagation is by means of cuttings, taken in spring and rooted in sandy soil in a warm propagating frame.

Acer negundo 'Variegatum'
Acer palmatum 'Sanguineum'
BOX ELDER AND JAPANESE MAPLE

These two fine maples are important not only on account of the colour they bring to flower borders and shrubberies, but because they are compact enough for small gardens. They belong to the natural order Aceraceae, a large family of deciduous trees, many of which are native to North America and East Asia.

Acer negundo is the North American box elder, a tree 12–21m (40–70ft) high; its wood is used for cheap furniture, packing cases and the like and its sap as a poor source of sugar. Its attractive cultivar 'Variegatum' however is much smaller-growing, 6m (20ft) or so in gardens, and certainly more conspicuous. The long-stalked, 15–25cm (6–10in), pinnate leaves have three or five leaflets, green irregularly bordered with white. Occasionally some leaves are entirely white. *Acer negundo* 'Variegatum' makes a good specimen tree on a lawn or can be used at the back of a border. In Victorian times it was popular for growing in pots in cool hallways or lofty rooms.

Acer palmatum 'Sanguineum' is one of many cultivars derived from the 6m (20ft) Japanese species *A. palmatum*. Its leaves are five-lobed and blood-red or crimson when young, becoming dark olive-green as they mature. The plant must be grown in a sheltered position, away from salt spray or strong drying winds and gales and does best in deep loam or peaty soil in light shade or full sun. Late frosts can cut the young foliage, and draughts can cause it to shrivel.

The propagation of coloured-leaved acers is usually carried out by grafting scions on stocks of their own green-leaved species. Air layering and ground layering may be tried, though both are often unsuccessful. However if they do grow the gardener will have plants on their own roots – and these never sucker. To make dwarf bushes suitable for pot work the grafts should be made very low down on the stock plant.

Agave americana 'Variegata'

VARIEGATED CENTURY PLANT

Few succulents are more impressive than a well-grown specimen of the variegated-leaved American aloe. A plant of striking habit, belonging to the natural order Agavaceae, it has grey-green, leathery leaves up to 1m (3ft) long and 12–15cm (5–6in) wide, each ending in a sharp spiny point. The margins are toothed, and broad, creamy, marginal bands run the length of every leaf. The leaves are arranged in a wide spreading rosette several feet across, above a stout, trunk-like stem. After some ten years American aloes bloom freely in hot climates, producing crowded panicles of greenish-yellow, lily-like flowers on rigid stems. In temperate countries however they take much longer, normally about thirty to forty years. For this reason they are frequently but erroneously called century plants. The flower spikes also vary in height between 6 and 12m (20–40ft) according to climate.

Strong fibres account for the rigidity of the leaves, a characteristic common to most aloes but particularly marked in *A. sisalana*, which produces the sisal hemp used for cordage. *A. americana* has a flax-like fibre, popular for drawn-thread work in the Azores. The Mexican national drink, pulque, is obtained from another species *A. atrovirens* (*Haworthis herbacea*). The inflorescences are removed as soon as they start to develop, which causes a sweet sap to ooze out. This is collected and fermented over a period of several months. The drug mecogenin, which can be converted into cortisone, occurs in the leaves of several species.

All agaves are frost tender, but benefit from being placed outside during the summer months. They should be grown in large, well-crocked pots or containers of sandy soil, and they are propagated by means of offsets. These should be removed and separately potted in spring. Seed is also used for increasing the species, but not the variegated-leaved forms.

Variegated-leaved aloes make striking specimen plants for raised jardinières, or can be used in sub-tropical bedding. Their sharp thorns command respect, so when repotting them twist newspaper round the leaves to protect the hands.

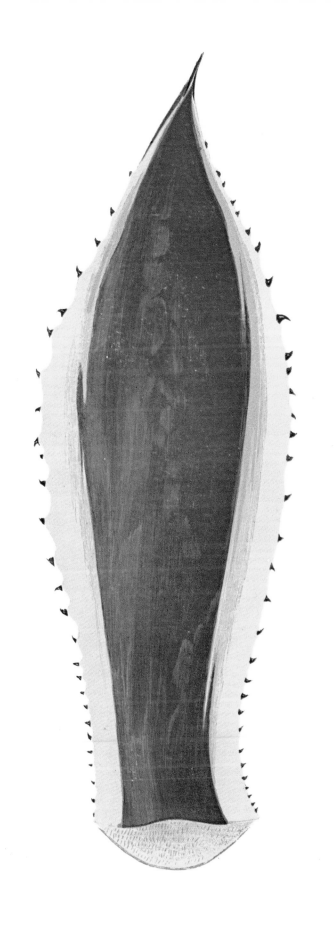

Alocasia lowii

TARO

This handsome plant comes from Borneo and was introduced to Britain by a nurseryman called Low in 1862. At that time it was believed to be a caladium and originally named *Caladium veitchii*, then *Caladium lowii*; but after having seen the flowers botanists determined the genus as alocasia, so the species should be called *Alocasia lowii*.

Like other alocasias it belongs to the natural order Araceae. It is an ever-green tropical perennial with a long rhizome and a short stem, sheathed around with the bases of its upright 30–40cm (12–16in) leafstalks. The arrow-shaped leaves grow 30–46cm (12–18in) long and 12–23cm (5–9in) wide, the base of each being divided by a deep opening into a pair of oblong lobes. The leaves are leathery in texture and olive-green in colour, with thick ivory-white ribs and deep purple beneath. The 10cm (4in) arum-like flowers are white.

To grow alocasias well they must be given plenty of warmth and humidity and abundant water during the growing season. *A. lowii* is accordingly more of a greenhouse subject than a room plant, although it can go outdoors for short periods. It should be grown in a large pot or container, crocked for a third of its depth and planted in a mixture of equal parts by bulk of fibrous loam (left rather lumpy) and fibrous peat, with additionally some coarse sand, chopped sphagnum moss, and a few lumps of charcoal. The tubers should be left just above the tops of the pots. Give the plants a weekly feed of fertilizer during the growing season and shade them from bright sunshine. Rest the tubers in winter. Appropriate temperatures are around 24–29c (75–85f) in summer and 15–18c (60–65f) in winter.

Propagation is by means of offsets attached to the parent plant. These should be removed and separately potted in spring.

Alocasia metallica

METALLIC ALOCASIA

Alocasia metallica, also known as *Alocasia cuprea*, is a rare but beautiful aroid which was first introduced to the west from its native Borneo in 1860. There are some seventy species in the genus, belonging to the natural order Araceae; all of them are tropical and some, like *Alocasia macrorrhiza* and *Alocasia cucullata*, the giant taro, cultivated for their edible rhizomes.

The plant portrayed is one of the most ornamental, with large, ovate-cordate, fleshy leaves 25–36cm (10–14in) across on 20–30cm (8–12in) smooth stems. The leaf colour is bronze-purple, with a metallic sheen which as it catches the light produces variable tints. The underside is deep violet. Like a chameleon the plant assumes different shades according to the amount of light which strikes the foliage; red, blue or purple tints follow each other upon the bronzy surface as the sun's rays reach them, producing magnificent effects.

The inflorescence is a green and purple (or sometimes white with purple at the tip) arum-like flower 6–9cm (2½–3½in) long. *Alocasia metallica* needs a coarse open compost and plenty of water whilst growing. Lumpy loam, fibrous peat and coarse sand in equal proportions should be well mixed with pieces of lump charcoal and chopped sphagnum moss. It is important to provide plenty of drainage so the pots should be two thirds full of crocks before any soil at all is added. Temperatures need to be high: 15–18c (60–65f) in winter and 21–24c (70–75f) in summer.

Propagation is not easy under home conditions. Seed, if produced, should be sown in small pots and germinated in a warm propagating frame. Otherwise, if suckers are produced they can be separated from the rhizome in early spring and grown on in a warm place.

Alternanthera amoena 'Sessilis'

PARROT LEAF

Also known as *Alternanthera sessilis* var. 'Amoena', this is a dwarf herbaceous perennial, native to Brazil. It belongs to the natural order Amaranthaceae, with 200 species, and its chief value to gardeners is for bedding-out purposes – particularly carpet-bedding, floral clocks and the like. The brightly-coloured foliage tolerates frequent clipping or pinching back to keep it dwarf, but when used for any form of bedding many plants are required since individual specimens are of little value and make no impact. The plant is also used by aquarists to provide colour in tropical aquaria – although the colour fades to green in time – and it is often grown with other house plants in mixed ornamental bowls for the home.

The lanceolate to elliptic leaves are small, 2.5–7.5cm (1–3in) long with slender pointed tips. Basically they are green with reddish-orange and reddish-purple veins and blotches, changing with age to shades of bronze and olive. Good leaf colours can only be obtained by growing the plants in a good bright light, for example in full sun outdoors or on a bright windowsill in the home. The brownish flowers are insignificant and usually picked off on sight.

Outdoors, alternantheras will grow in any reasonably good, well-drained soil in sheltered situations; indoors they can be grown in John Innes potting compost, or in a made-up soil mix composed of equal parts by bulk of sifted loam, peat and sand. For propagating details see *Alternanthera versicolor* (plate 8).

The species is widespread in the tropics where it is known as racaba. Its leaves are eaten as a vegetable in Malaya, cooked with rice dishes in Indonesia and with fish in Zaire.

Alternanthera versicolor

COPPER ALTERNANTHERA

Also known as *Teleianthera ficoidea* var. *versicolor*, or more affectionately as joyweed, this charming little plant comes from Brazil and belongs to the natural order Amaranthaceae. It is one of several species commonly used by parks authorities in the making of carpet-bedding, including floral clocks. Tolerant of frequent clipping or pinching back, it makes a good bright background for this kind of gardening. But the species may also be grown as a pot-plant or mixed with others in indoor containers. When allowed to develop naturally it then makes a small shrubby specimen, 20–25cm (8–10in) high, with oval, opposite leaves of pale carmine, deep bronze-red, claret colour and rose-pink, together with two or three shades of green. In order to retain the brighter shades it is necessary to grow the plants in very good light and pinch them back frequently, as the young foliage is the most colourful. The flowers are insignificant and should be removed on sight as they detract from the leaves. Joyweeds are not winter hardy where frosts prevail so they must be lifted and potted in late summer in cool climates and kept in a heated frame or greenhouse all winter. Temperatures at that time should be around 15c (60f) or over.

Keep the·plants fairly dry in winter and then in spring apply water more freely in order to encourage shoot growth. Some of these shoots can be removed for cuttings if required. Alternatively cuttings can be taken in August, rooted in boxes and kept under glass until the following spring before being potted.

Alternantheras are not easy plants to keep through the winter, for if over-watered or allowed to get cold they rot at the base. So a few plants should always be kept in a heated frame or centrally-heated room indoors to maintain the stock.

A. versicolor makes an attractive edging for plant boxes in centrally-heated rooms.

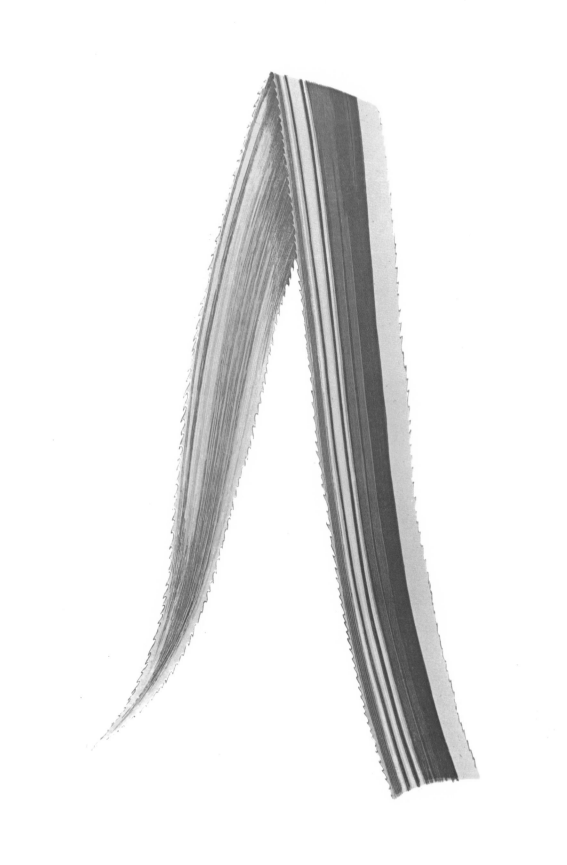

Ananas comosus 'Variegatus'

VARIEGATED-LEAVED PINEAPPLE

This is a variegated-leaved form of one of the world's favourite fruits – the pineapple. It belongs to the natural order Bromeliaceae and like many members of that family makes an excellent house plant. Columbus was the first European to discover the species – on the island of Guadeloupe in 1493. It grows wild in Brazil and several other South American countries. Horace Walpole, writing in 1780, states that the first pineapple fruit grown in England was presented to Charles II by his gardener Rose in 1685.

Ananas comosus is a terrestrial bromeliad with narrow, arching, spiny-edged leaves up to 1m (3ft) in length arranged in a rosette which may be 1m (3ft) across. These are plain green in the type, but in the variety 'Variegatus' they have bold yellow stripes and, when grown in a good light, rosy-pink suffusions.

The flowers arise from the centre of the leaf rosettes in a dense spike with purplish petals and short stamens, the bracts and upper leaves being a rich rosy-red. Under good conditions plants produce fruits after two or three years, when suckers develop around the sides of the parent plant, which then dies. The suckers can then be removed for propagating purposes. To grow satisfactory pineapples good light and warm temperatures 18–21c (65–70f) in summer and around 15–18c (60–65f) in winter are essential. The plants need rich compost, consisting of one part (by bulk) leafmould, two parts fibrous loam, a half part well-decomposed manure, and a quarter part peat. Crock the pots well and plant in spring; repot them in late summer if necessary.

Propagation is effected by removing the suckers when they reach a convenient size for handling. Allow them to lie on a shelf for 24 hours to dry up the wound before planting. Keep the pots in a warm propagating frame but refrain from giving them much water until they root.

Anoectochilus discolor 'Rubro-venia'

JEWEL ORCHID

The species *Anoectochilus discolor*, of which 'Rubro-venia' is a form, belongs to the natural order Orchidaeae. There are about 25 species in the genus, mostly native to tropical Asia, Australia and Polynesia. *A. discolor*, also known as *Haemaria discolor* and *Goodyera discolor*, is one of the most successful species of anoectochilus in cultivation with sturdy, rather fleshy stems, and dark, velvety, reddish-green leaves 5–8cm (2–3in) long and 2.5–3cm (1–1$\frac{1}{4}$in) wide; each of which has a central whitish stripe and a few bright red veins. The shape is ovate with pointed tips. The form known as 'Rubro-venia' has red veins only (no white), one of which runs down the centre and one on each side. These curve towards the margins and meet at the centre vein near the top of the leaf. The pinkish-green flowers, though pretty, lack horticultural import-ance, being somewhat small. Several of them grow together on 5–7.5cm (2–3in) stems.

The plant should be grown in equal parts by bulk of sphagnum moss and chopped osmunda fern (or fibrous peat), with a few finely crushed flower-pot crocks and charcoal, and a small quantity of dried oak leaves and fibrous loam. Half-fill the pots with broken crocks and after planting give little or no water until the plants start to grow, then add more gradually. Keep shaded from sunshine and away from draughts.

The plant is increased, by division of the creeping stems, into as many parts as there are shoots with attached roots. Pot these shoots and keep them in a closed propagating frame until they recover from the move.

Although this species is easier to increase than most members of the genus, it is rare and highly prized. Temperature as for *A. regalis* (plate 11).

Anoectochilus regalis

ROYAL JEWEL ORCHID

Also known as *Anoectochilus setaceus*, and king plant, this beautiful example comes from Sri-Lanka (Ceylon) and was introduced to Kew Gardens in 1836. Its chief charm lies in its rounded-ovate, exquisitely-marked leaves, which are each about 5cm (2in) long and 4cm (1½in) wide. The colour is velvety-green with a metallic lustre, the whole surface intersected with a network of golden, reddish lines. When examined under a microscope, with the sun shining full upon the leaves, the veins appear rich beyond description. It is a variable species from which a number of forms have been selected. Several flowers are borne on each 10cm (4in) stem. The greenish upper sepals and petals of each bloom form a hood with spreading lateral sepals, above a white, fimbriated, claw-like petal spur at the back.

In nature the species is found in shady places growing on decomposed vegetation and rock debris, which the creeping stem and roots can readily penetrate.

Anoectochilus species are not easy plants to cultivate and must be kept away from draughts and direct sunlight. A moist warm atmosphere 21c (70F) or over in summer and 15–18c (60–65F) in winter is necessary, particularly when they are growing. Some people find the plants thrive inside glass containers, for example in a carboy garden or under a cloche or small frame in a greenhouse. Excess moisture must be avoided if this seems likely to drop on the leaves. Cultivate and propagate as for *A. discolor* (plate 10).

Aucuba japonica 'Maculata'

GOLD DUST TREE

Aucubas, often but erroneously called laurels, are Japanese hardy evergreen shrubs belonging to the natural order Cornaceae. They were particularly popular in Victorian times for making dense 2–3m (8–10ft) hedges, and for pot culture. At that time only female plants were known and because the sexes are on different plants these never berried. And then, around 1864, Robert Fortune introduced a male plant, pollen from which applied to some female flowers resulted in the latter bearing heavy crops of rich scarlet berries. This caused such excitement in the gardening world that suddenly everyone wanted to grow aucubas. The demand for male plants was immense, some of the early plants produced costing a small fortune. But there was no difficulty in selling them. The only problem was to multiply them fast enough, every available bud being used for grafting purposes.

Nowadays it is easy to reproduce either sex, from cuttings taken in late summer, out of doors.

Aucubas are excellent shrubs for shady situations and if both male and female plants are grown the females berry up without trouble. However, pot-grown specimens have to be hand-pollinated – transferring the pollen from a male flower to a female with a camel-hair brush. Berried aucubas make handsome plants for cool rooms indoors, especially in winter. During the summer months they should be plunged in soil outdoors, up to their rims and in light shade.

Aucubas will grow in any good garden soil outdoors and in any proprietary compost or soil mix in pots. Plants should be watered freely in summer, sparingly in winter and fed monthly with a liquid fertilizer during the summer months.

There are a number of cultivars with variously-shaped leaves. Several have foliage variegations, like 'Maculata' (the plant portrayed) and another called 'Variegata', both having broad splashes of yellow on their leaves. And some varieties have yellow instead of red berries.

Begonia rex

REX BEGONIA

The family Begoniaceae to which this plant belongs commemorates M. Michel Begon (1638–1710), an enthusiastic botanist and one time Governor of French Canada. The family is a large one, comprising some five genera, 920 species and countless cultivars. Amongst those grown primarily for their foliage *Begonia rex* is one of the most important, the large multicoloured leaves coming in a wide variety of shades and patternings.

Rex means 'king' and for many people *Begonia rex* is the king of begonias. It comes from Assam and is one of our best ornamental foliage plants, its beautiful leaves and compact habit a joy to behold. It is not difficult to cultivate provided, first, that it is not overwatered (which causes the stem bases to rot), and second, that it is kept in a temperature range of 15–21c (60–70F) whilst growing. Plants should also be rested for part of the year, and protected from strong sunlight.

Begonia rex has spreading rhizomatous roots and should be planted in pans or pots wide enough to take their spread. Since growth is seldom more than 23cm (9in) high, a front-row position is desirable in mixed collections of house plants.

The species was introduced in 1858 and has since produced many richly-coloured, vividly-marked cultivars. Most plants bear both male and female flowers on bristly stems, usually but not necessarily on the same spike. They are soft pink in colour. The leaves are obliquely ovate with heart-shaped bases 20–30cm (8–12in) in length and 15–20cm (6–8in) wide on red hairy stems.

Each leaf is beautifully patterned, basically dark green, with a broad greenish-white inner zone following the contours of the margins.

The whole surface has a metallic sheen and is bristly to the touch.

Cultivation requirements are identical with that of *B. rex* 'Nebulosa' (plate 15). The leaves – and in some cases flowers – of begonias are used locally in their native South America for reducing fevers and as a specific against colds. The leaves of *B. sanguinea* are also eaten, raw and cooked.

Begonia rex 'Grandis'

REX BEGONIA VARIETY

This is one of countless cultivars derived from the species *Begonia rex*. It is a plant of spreading habit growing about 30cm (1ft) high with oblong-oblique, heart-shaped leaves approximately 20cm (8in) long and 15cm (6in) wide, beautifully patterned in silvery-white and brownish olive-green, the lighter part spreading across the leaves in a broad irregular zone. Both stems and leaves are spangled with scarlet hairs tipped with white, the undersides of the leaves being rich crimson. The flowers are pink.

Like all *Begonia rex* cultivars, the plant can be propagated from leaf-cuttings by the method described on page xiii of the Introduction. Short hair-pins are excellent for this purpose. Give a gentle watering and place in a propagating case, or cover the box with a sheet of glass to maintain humidity. Bottom temperatures of 21c (70F) plus are necessary to induce rooting from the areas of the cuts. Soon small leaves and roots will appear at these spots and when large enough to handle the young plantlets can be separately potted in the soil mix recommended on page x of the Introduction or in compost made up from equal parts by bulk of peat moss, leafmould, coarse sand and sifted loam. Cultivation then follows the procedure recommended for *Begonia rex* 'Nebulosa' (plate 15).

Begonia rex 'Nebulosa'
REX BEGONIA CULTIVAR

Many *B. rex* cultivars have been derived from crossings with other species, notably *B. diadema*, indicated by jagged edges to the leaves, and *B. decora*. The size of the leaf varies according to cultivation, between 18–30cm (7–12in) across, the shape being an asymmetric oval or heart shape, with a short hairy stem which rarely exceeds 23cm (9in) in height attached to one side. The flowers are pretty but not showy, usually yellowish-white or pink and the roots rhizomatous with a tendency to spread outwards and over the edges of pots.

In cool climates *B. rex* cultivars are normally cultivated in the home or in a greenhouse, a temperature around 15c (60F) being ideal. All of them dislike strong sunlight, although a good light is essential if the colours are not to fade.

Use a lime-free but organic potting soil, one containing plenty of peat to retain moisture and give the roots a cool run. The mix recommended on page x of the Introduction is ideal, or one of the loamless composts sold by garden shops. Do not pot the plants too firmly and water them carefully at all times, using soft water for preference and keeping it off the leaves. In winter the plants should be kept as dry as possible – but not dust-dry – to provide them with a resting period. In early spring developing leaves will indicate the need for more water, which naturally should be applied more copiously in warm rooms.

Do not repot unless the plants are rootbound. Propagate from leaf-cuttings as described on page xiii of the Introduction. The cultivar portrayed, *B. rex* 'Nebulosa', is beautifully patterned in green, white, red and silver with each white spot set off by a single red hair.

Caladium bicolor 'Chantinii'

CALADIUM

Caladiums are tropical South American aroids with large, fleshy, rhizomatous roots. *Caladium bicolor* is one of the most important species since its boiled, ginger-like rhizomes are eaten as food in tropical countries under the name of cocoa roots, while an emetic and purgative medicine is extracted from the fresh rhizomes. The species, which is also known as *Arum bicolor*, is extremely variable with many cultivars, some of which make popular greenhouse foliage plants. The form portrayed was introduced and named for the French nursery-man M. Chantin in 1857.

It is a strong-growing, tuberous-rooted herbaceous plant about 80cm (32in) high with broad arrow-shaped leaves 35cm (14in) long by 25cm (10in) wide in the broadest part. These are deep crimson in the centre, shading off to pale green towards the margins and spangled with a profusion of irregular-sized and shaped white spots. The leaf stems are 60cm (2ft) high, dark purple in colour and striped with crimson.

Each spring the plants are started from dormant tubers, which are placed in chopped sphagnum moss or moist peat in a propagating frame, with bottom heat around 21–24c (70–75f). They should be sprayed daily until they begin to sprout; then potted (or repotted) in a mixture of equal parts by bulk of sandy loam, fibrous peat, rotted cow-manure and leafmould. If cow-manure is unavailable use a quarter part coarse bonemeal instead and then add enough coarse sand to make the mixture open and porous. Use the compost fairly dry and pot the tubers in small but well-crocked pots. Keep the plants warm and spray them over with soft water two or three times daily if possible.

Water sparingly at first and then more liberally as growth increases. Too much water induces rotting. Keep the plants away from draughts but give them plenty of light – but not direct sunlight – to bring out the rich leaf colours. Towards autumn, when the leaves start to fade, reduce the water gradually until the foliage has died down, then keep the pots in a frost-free place until the following spring. For propagation see *Caladium humboldtii* (plate 18).

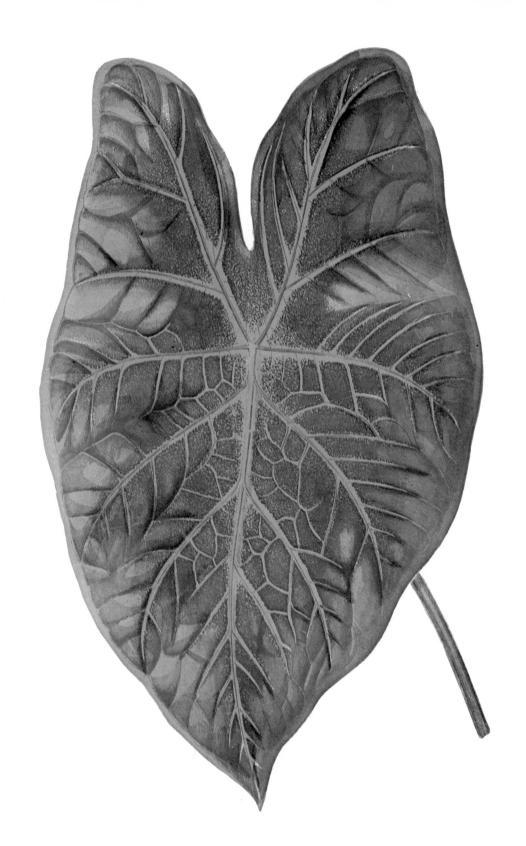

Caladium bicolor 'Splendens'

FANCY-LEAVED CALADIUM

The species *Caladium bicolor* is the most popular and variable species in the genus and the parent of dozens of cultivars commonly known as 'fancy-leaved caladiums'.

Caladium bicolor 'Splendens', also known as *Caladium roseum* and *C. splendens*, came to Europe via Madeira from its native South America in 1773. It is a deciduous herbaceous plant whose foliage disappears in winter and attains a height of around 60cm (2ft). When well grown the arrow-shaped leaves are about 23cm (9in) long and 18cm (7in) broad, the centre of each crimson-scarlet with a metallic lustre, the mid-vein and primary veins red-purple, and the margins and areas between the veins green. Under good conditions white arum-like flowers are produced. These are monoecious, the female blooms ripening first, so that to produce seeds it is necessary to cut away part of the spathe and hand-pollinate them. The seedlings have green leaves at first, the gaudy colouring not developing until the plants make six or seven leaves. The results are also extremely variable, so cultivars like 'Splendens' are best propagated from the small tubers which grow from the sides of mature tubers, as described under *Caladium humboldtii* (plate 18).

The plants should lie dormant in winter, and in spring have all the old soil removed, before being repotted half an inch deep in a mixture of peat, turfy loam and well-rotted cow-manure (in equal parts by bulk). The pots should have plenty of drainage and go into a propagating frame with bottom heat, but they should be given no water until the leaves begin to appear. They can then be watered as necessary until autumn when they can be gradually dried off and stored away from moisture and frost. Temperatures around 21–26c (70–80F) in summer and 13–15c (55–60F) in winter are ideal.

Caladium humboldtii

HUMBOLDT'S CALADIUM

This plant, also known as *Caladium argyrites* and *C. lilliputiense,* is another of the South American aroids introduced by M. Chantin of Paris in 1857. There are about fifteen species in the genus – all South American, in the natural order Araceae.

Caladium humboldtii is a small and graceful, tuberous-rooted herbaceous perennial about 45cm (1½ft) high with comparatively small, arrow-shaped leaves. These are light green with white centres and margins, and they have many irregular, almost transparent, white spots between the veins. The leaf-stalks are two or three times as long as the leaves, which gives the plant a peculiar grace and makes it suitable for table decoration.

Like all caladiums the tubers need resting in winter. The plants are intolerant of wet soil, so should not be overpotted or overwatered. Grow them as recommended for *Caladium bicolor* 'Chantinii' (plate 16). Frequent watering with liquid manure whilst they are in full leaf helps to produce good foliage.

In northern Europe propagation is usually vegetative as seed is difficult to come by. When the tubers grow large enough they produce smaller ones along their sides. These can be carefully detached, and after leaving them to dry a little while to heal the wounds, they can be separately potted. Dusting the cuts with powdered charcoal prevents decay on both large and small tubers. This operation is best carried out in early spring, when the small potted tubers should be packed in a box of chopped sphagnum peat and covered with an inch of the same material until they sprout. Meantime keep them in a propagating frame with bottom heat temperatures around 24–29c (75–85f).

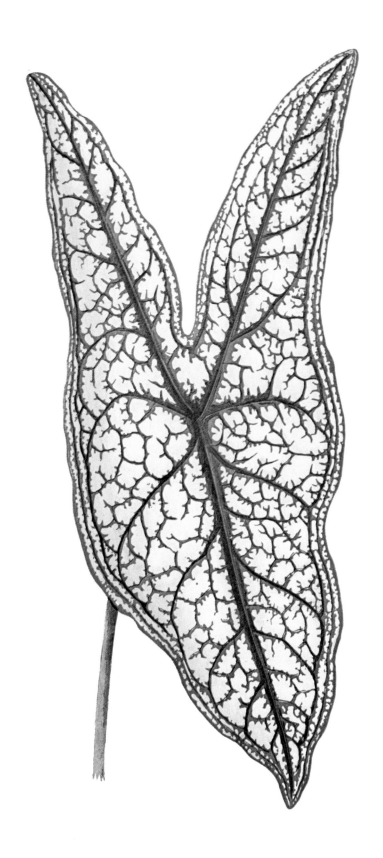

Caladium picturatum 'Belleymei'

PAINTED CALADIUM

This is one of the most remarkable of the series of caladiums collected in Para, Brazil by the collector Baraquin, and subsequently introduced to Europe by M. Chantin of Paris.

The cultivar 'Belleymei' is one of the finest of the fancy-leaved caladiums, its sharply sagittate leaves being almost wholly a translucent white, excepting for green veins and nerves and small green spots along the margins with occasional suffusions of pale rose. The leaf-stalks are green at the tops but variegated with violet lower down. The average height of the whole plant is approximately 86cm (34in).

Although caladiums are grown as foliage plants they do occasionally flower under good cultural conditions. The blooms resemble arums and are usually white or greenish, although scarcely ornamental. Male and female flowers are arranged separately on the spadix, those at the top being exclusively male and pollen-bearing; those at the base female. Since the latter ripen first it is sometimes necessary to hand-pollinate the blooms if seed is required.

This cultivar requires shade from sun, a temperature of 21–26c (70–80f) and abundant atmospheric moisture. It does best in a humid greenhouse. In a centrally-heated house it should be placed on a gravel tray which always has a little water at the bottom. Annual repotting is essential, the compost being of a loamy or peaty nature, rich in vegetable fibre. When the tubers are started in the early part of the year, it is advisable to plunge the pots in some moist material – such as sphagnum moss or peat – in a larger container and water into the latter rather than directly into the plant pots, until the tubers are well sprouted.

Failures occur most frequently in winter, rather than summer, usually because the tubers are kept too hot or too cold. Temperatures around 13c (55f) are most suitable at this period.

Calathea roseo-picta

ROSY ARROWROOT

Calatheas are tropical plants from southern and central America and the West Indies. They take their name from the Greek *kalathos*, a basket, a reference to the flower clusters which come in short spikes set off by the leathery bracts, so that they look something like flowers in a basket. They belong to the monocotyledonous family Marantaceae and are of varying habit, often with strikingly patterned leaves. The flowers are generally small and insignificant.

Calatheas are normally grown as house plants, preferably in centrally-heated homes where constant warmth and humidity can be maintained. Strong light should be avoided as it makes the leaves curl and temperatures should not fall below 10c (50F). Standing the pots on gravel trays with a little water in their bases, or plunging them in larger pots full of moist peat ensure the 'under foliage' dampness essential to their well-being. They will also grow within the close confines of a bottle garden.

Browning at the leaf tips is usually an indication of prolonged drought at the roots or waterlogging. An open compost, containing plenty of organic material, is accordingly essential and a recommended mix is equal parts, by bulk, of light loam, leafmould and peat plus one-third part of sharp sand.

Propagation is effected by careful division of the roots in early spring, when the young disturbed plantlets should be kept in the close atmosphere of a warm propagating frame until they re-establish.

Calathea roseo-picta, which is also known as *Maranta roseo-picta*, is a native of Brazil. It is of dwarf habit, growing a mere 20cm (8in) high, with 2.5cm (1in) long, short-stalked leaves which are unequally sided and handsomely veined. Their colour is green with bright rosy midribs and irregular bands of ruby and white between these and the margins. The undersides of the leaves are purplish.

Calathea rotundifolia var. fasciata
ROUND-LEAVED CALATHEA

There are about 150 calatheas belonging to the natural order Marantaceae, and some have economic properties. *C. allovia*, for example, is known as sweet root-corn in the West Indies because of its edible bulbs from which Guinea arrowroot is obtained. The young plants of *C. violacea* and *C. macrosepala* are used as vegetables, and the tough leaves of *C. discolor* are waterproof when dried and often used for thatching. The plant portrayed here, also known as *Maranta fasciata*, comes from Brazil. It grows up to 30cm (12in) high and has nearly round leaves about 15cm (6in) across and 20cm (8in) wide on 9cm (3½in) stems. The leaves of var. *fasciata* are dark olive-green with transverse bars of silvery-white, reaching from the midribs nearly to the margin. The undersides are dull-grey green, occasionally slightly shaded with crimson. The flowers are a transparent white, in a nearly round, stalkless spike, set off by brownish bracts.

A healthy plant eventually makes a large showy specimen, so plant it in a large, well-crocked pot with a rich growing medium. Equal parts by bulk of fibrous loam, sandy peat, well-decomposed cow-manure (or a quarter part coarse bonemeal), or garden compost, the whole mixed with a sprinkling of sand, makes an ideal compost. Finally topdress the pot with granite chips or lightweight fuel ash pellets (sold as Lytag or Hortag) to prevent too much damp round the collar. Water as required, keep the foliage clean, and provide humidity by standing the pot on gravel with water at the base – almost but not quite touching the base of the pot.

Calathea rotundifolia var. *fasciata* requires temperatures of up to 26c (80F) in summer and 21c (70F) in winter. Like most calatheas it may need annual repotting to prevent foliage overcrowding. Propagation and cultivation are as recommended for *Calathea roseo-picta* (plate 20).

43

Calathea veitchiana

VEITCH'S CALATHEA

Calathea veitchiana was named in honour of the great nineteenth-century nurseryman James Veitch, whose numerous plant introductions included many from South America. The leaves are ovate-elliptic in shape, about 14cm (5½in) long and 9cm (3½in) across and rounded at the base with maroon undersides and a feathering of light green, emerald, and dark green patterning above. It is native to Venezuela.

The plant requires warm temperatures around 13–21c (55–70F) in summer and 13–15c (55–60F) in winter; also rich compost, consisting of two parts by bulk fibrous loam, two parts sandy peat, one part rotted manure and one part leafmould. These ingredients should be liberally intermixed with enough sharp sand to give the resultant compost porosity. A few pieces of lump charcoal help to keep the mixture sweet.

In summer water freely, in winter very sparingly. Repot in March if necessary and if you have a propagating frame plunge the pots in this for a short while to help the plants to get over the move. Marantas are good plants for centrally-heated homes, where temperatures are fairly constant. Propagation and cultivation are as for *Calathea roseo-picta* (plate 20).

Calathea vittata

RIBBONED MARANTA

The ribboned maranta, *Calathea vittata*, previously known as *Maranta vittata*, comes from Colombia, and was introduced in 1857. It is a handsome evergreen perennial with long oval, or oblong-lanceolate leaves which have tapering points. These are thin-textured and very variable in size, but on average about 20cm (8in) long on 10cm (4in) stout downy stems. The colour is light green, with symmetrical narrow, transverse, silvery-white stripes each side of the midrib. It is one of the handsomest species in the genus, because this variegation remains constant throughout the year.

The plant sends out side-shoots or offsets, which when rooted can be detached with a sharp knife and potted in the recommended soil mixture. They should then be kept in the close atmosphere of a propagating frame until they become established; after which they can be taken out and treated as established plants. Cultivation is as for *Calathea roseo-picta* (plate 20).

Calathea warscewiczii

WARSCEWICZ'S ARROWROOT

Also known as *Maranta warscewiczii*, this beautiful leaved plant takes its name from Joseph Warscewicz (1812–66), a Polish botanist. The species is a strong-growing evergreen perennial with 30cm (12in) stems each carrying a broad lanceolate or oblong-lanceolate leaf 30–45cm (12–18in) long and 10–15cm (4–6in) wide. These are sharp-pointed and rich, dark green with paler green, feathery patternings each side of the midrib. The undersides are purple. The species comes from Costa Rica.

It is less difficult to grow than many other species in this genus provided it is not kept too cold. Temperatures around 21c (70F) in summer and 15–18c (60–65F) in winter are ideal.

Propagation is effected by separating the sturdier side-shoots, potting these in the soil mix recommended for *Calathea rotundifolia* var. *fasciata* (plate 21), and keeping them in a warm propagating frame until they root.

Canna indica Hybrid

INDIAN SHOT

The genus *Canna*, with 55 species, is the sole member of the natural order Cannaceae. All are native to tropical and sub-tropical America and have large fleshy roots which are eaten as food by some Colombian and Ecuadorian Indians. The large simple leaves bear some resemblance to those of the banana and the funnel-shaped flowers are borne on terminal inflorescences. The leaves may be plain green, reddish-purple or green overlaid with red and are approximately 75cm (2½ft) long by 25cm (10in) wide and stoutly ribbed. The brilliant flowers on 1.2m (4ft) spikes come in hot shades of scarlet, apricot, vivid orange, coral rose or deep yellow – either self-coloured, or spotted or suffused with other shades. The individual blooms have only three sepals and three petals but since the showy stamens have petal-like appendages of similar colour, the blooms have a many-petalled appearance.

The first attempt to use cannas as sub-tropical bedding plants in temperate latitudes was made by M. Année, a French consular agent in Chile in 1846. The various sorts he planted in his garden at Passy were so successful that he commenced systematically to cross the various kinds available and the results laid the foundation of the splendid collections now grown in European gardens, especially those of the south.

Cannas can be grown from seed but these need soaking for 24 hours prior to sowing as they have an exceptionally hard seed-coat – a circumstance which retards germination and presumably accounts for them being given the popular name of Indian Shot. Named cultivars however must be propagated vegetatively by splitting the fleshy rhizomes in spring and potting the divisions in fibrous peat or leafy soil. They should then be kept in a warm temperature (around 15c (60F)) to get them growing.

One species of canna, *C. edulis*, is the source of Queensland arrowroot, an invalid food, while the leaves of many species are used in South America for wrapping fish and other foods.

Cissus discolor

BEGONIA TREE-BINE

Climbing evergreen vines are invaluable for home decoration and one of the most beautiful is the magnificent Javanese *Cissus discolor*. Introduced to Europe in 1851, it belongs to the natural order Vitaceae with about 350 species in the genus. The specific name is very apt for *discolor* means 'of different and distinct colours', an epithet borne out by the foliage patterning. The leaves are simple, cordate-lanceolate with pointed tips, up to 15cm (6in) in length and 8cm (3in) across with a velvety texture, the upper surface being rich olive-green, marbled with white and rich purple, the edges and main veins purple and the leaf-blade shaded with white, peach and crimson. The undersides of the leaves are a rich brownish-crimson.

These beautiful leaves come on strong stems, which are red when young but later become brown and woody. However, *Cissus discolor* is not as easy to grow as some of the green-leaved members of the genus, like *Cissus rhombifolia* and the kangaroo vine, *Cissus antarctica*, both of which stand fairly low temperatures and are common in cultivation. *Cissus discolor* requires warmth, and temperatures should not fall below 13c (55F) in winter. Indeed, 18–21c (65–70F) would be better.

The plant can be trained up supports or encouraged to grow across the walls of a warm room. It can also be kept compact if trained around wire or cane shapes or even allowed to trail from the sides of a hanging basket. The tropical waterlily house at the Royal Botanic Gardens in Kew has some splendid examples of plants growing in this manner. Shade from strong sunlight is necessary as this destroys the rich leaf colouring and for the same reason water must not touch the leaves. Avoid hard water and overwatering, which cause mildew and brown spots on the foliage.

A good growing medium is John Innes Compost No. 1, or equal parts by bulk of loam, coarse sand, well-rotted manure and leafmould with a half part peat, the whole mixed together with a small quantity of superphosphate and bonemeal (half pint) per barrow load.

Propagation is by means of cuttings rooted in two parts peat and one part sharp sand in a warm propagating frame with bottom heat, around 24c(75F).

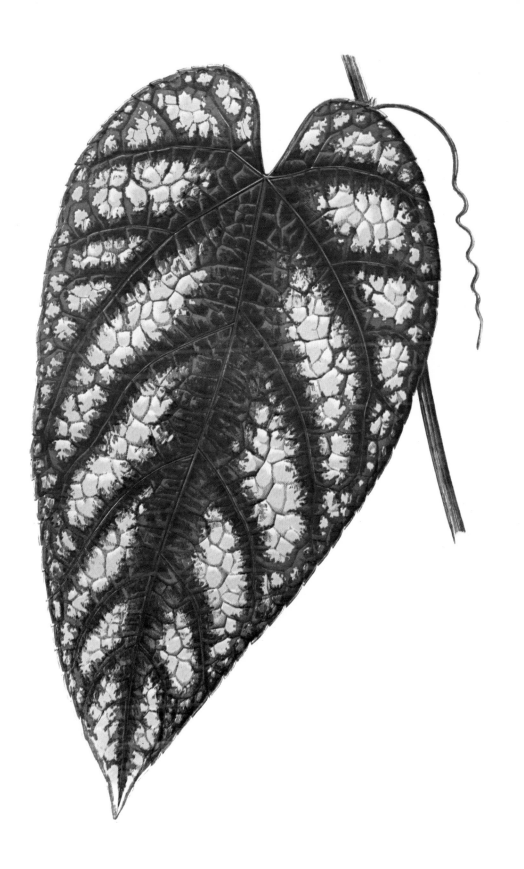

Coleus blumei

FLAME NETTLE

Among the most spectacular foliage plants for pot work or summer bedding are the many varieties of *Coleus blumei*, or flame nettles as they are popularly known. They are easy to grow and multiply, and cheap to buy, while their varied and brilliant multicoloured leaves form a striking contrast to both silver and green foliaged plants as well as to flowers of pale tints.

There are about 150 species of coleus, some herbaceous, some shrubby, all originating in Asia or Africa and all belonging to the natural order Labiatae. Those most widely-grown however are varieties derived from *Coleus blumei* and these occur in a wide range of shades. A single packet of seed will produce as many different varieties as seedlings. When plant hybridists first started to experiment with the species amateur horticulturalists were enthralled with the results. Quite a small package of different sorts was auctioned in 1868 for £402 8s. – a vast sum for the times.

Cuttings of desirable sorts root easily at any time between early spring and midsummer, either in John Innes Seed Compost or a mixture of equal parts by bulk of sharp sand and peat fibre. Insert the cuttings singly in small pots, or in seed trays if large quantities are involved. Coleus cuttings will also root in water in a dark container, but need potting directly afterwards. Pot all the young plants once or twice after rooting in John Innes No. 1 Potting Compost and stop them once by pinching out the growing tip of the shoot. This will make for strong, bushy, fibrous-rooted plants. Harden off the young plants if they are to go outside, and in any case do not plant them in the garden until there is no longer any risk of frost.

Indoors, coleus must have plenty of light or the leaves will fade, revert to green, or (if the light is very poor) drop. Coleus dislike lime so should never be given limy compost or watered with hard water. The soil ball must not dry out or the plant will collapse and die. During the growing season plenty of water is necessary, and occasional feeds with a lime-free fertilizer.

Convallaria majalis 'Variegata'

VARIEGATED-LEAVED LILY OF THE VALLEY

The lily of the valley is not only the national flower of Finland but a universal favourite on account of its charming little flowers and sweet penetrating scent. It is a monotypic genus belonging to the natural order Liliaceae, with a wide distribution throughout Europe, including Britain (but excluding the extreme north and south), temperate Asia and North America.

The plant is an herbaceous perennial with a creeping rhizomatous rootstock, long-stalked, elliptic-lanceolate leaves 12–18cm (5–7in) long and 4cm (1½in) wide which occur in pairs and arching 15–20cm (6–8in) flower stems carrying between five and eight drooping white 1.5cm (½in) six-lobed, bell-shaped flowers with turned up edges. It blooms in early summer and persists in character for several weeks. There are a number of cultivated forms, including one with rosy-lilac flowers called 'Rosea', two doubles, one of which carries its blossoms in a single row, the other having clusters of flowers like bunches of grapes, and 'Variegata' which is the subject of our illustration. This form is particularly fine for its leaves are striped longitudinally with golden lines from base to apex and remain attractive for months – long after the flowers have faded. All the cultivars are in general cultivation.

The striped lily of the valley is of easy culture and takes more sun than the green-leaved species. If grown in too much shade the variegation disappears; if this occurs the plain leaves should be removed. It does best in poor sandy loam. It is lime-tolerant but it dislikes wet, heavy ground. An occasional dressing with well-rotted leaf soil encourages the plant to spread.

Lilies of the valley have a few economic properties. The dried rhizomes have been used medicinally as a heart tonic and diuretic. Lily of the valley water, known in Europe as Aqua Aurea, is made from the flowers and at one time was considered so precious that it was kept in vessels of gold or silver. The plant was also an ingredient of love potions and because it bloomed at that time became particularly associated with Whitsuntide.

Other English names once applied to lily of the valley include lily constancy, Our Lady's tears, mugget and glovewort – the last because the sap was recommended 'for sore hands'.

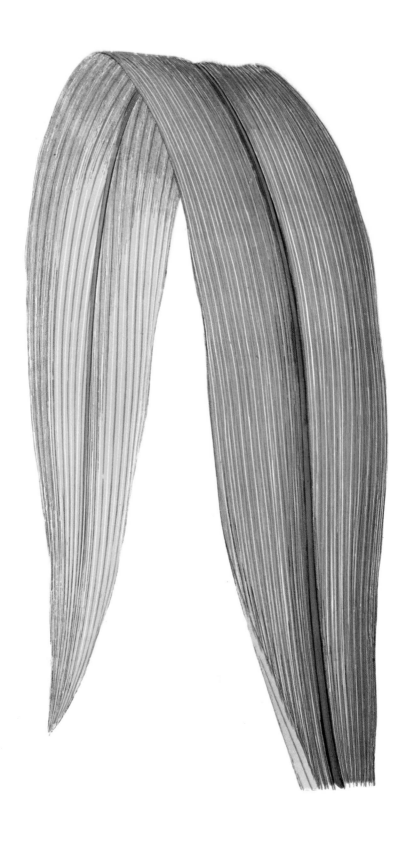

Cordyline indivisa

BLUE DRACAENA

This beautiful cordyline comes from New Zealand. It is one of approximately fifteen species of dracaena-like plants belonging to the natural order Agavaceae. All are natives of tropical or warm temperate climates, although a few – including *Cordyline indivisa* – can be grown outside in mild, sheltered, near frost-free situations.

Given good conditions it makes a small tree, rarely more than 3m (10ft) tall, with an erect trunk and terminal heads of thick, leathery and elegant sword-shaped leaves 1–2m (3–6ft) long and 15cm (6in) wide. These are green with yellowish midribs. Dropping panicles of tiny, closely-packed, white and purple flowers occur on 60cm–1.3m (2–4ft) trusses.

The cultivar portrayed here originated from a seedling raised in 1852 by Messrs. Lee of Hammersmith. It is doubtful if it is still in cultivation, but as the illustration reveals it was a plant with remarkable leaf colouring. The overall hue is rich bronzy-green, the midrib crimson-brown and there are many red and white stripes running the whole length of the leaf.

Small cordylines make impressive container plants in places where there is room for the leaves to spread and develop. A compost of loam and lumpy peat (in equal proportions by bulk) with a little sand suits them well and they benefit from a sojourn outdoors during the summer months. Plenty of water is required during the growing season, although the quantity can be reduced in winter so as to keep the soil just moist. All the variegated kinds need plenty of light to bring out their colouring.

Occasionally plants send up basal suckers and these can be taken off and potted when firm for propagation purposes. For large quantities it is usual to sacrifice a specimen and cut up its stems into pieces of 2–5cm (1–2in) and root these in sandy soil in a warm propagating frame.

Fibres from the leaves of *Cordyline indivisa* were once used by Maoris for the making of garments and by early settlers in place of twine. The leaves have also been used in paper-making and, according to R. M. Laing (*Plants of New Zealand*), when decayed become phosphorescent at night.

Cordyline terminalis

RED DRACAENA

This is a plant from southern Asia and Polynesia belonging to the natural order Agavaceae. It is highly popular for indoor cultivation, particularly in mixed bowls of house plants and, although not hardy, is sometimes used in warm sheltered situations for emphasis among summer-bedding.

The plant is a palm-like, evergreen shrub with a cane-like trunk which in nature runs up to 3m (10ft), but is more generally seen 1–1.3m (3–4ft) in height when grown in containers. The rather slender, leathery-textured, sword-shaped leaves, each about 30cm (12in) long and 10cm (4in) wide, grow and spread outwards in bold clusters from the tops of the trunks and are of a rich purplish-red with a crimson midrib when young. As they age the brilliance fades to a copper-red. There are a number of cultivars of which 'Firebrand' is especially brilliant. 'Guilfoylei' has red, white and pink stripes on a greenish background and is all white towards the lower part of its leaves.

The species likes rich soil and plenty of moisture while growing. Rochford recommends a compost made up from 6 parts by bulk of loam with 5 of peat, 4 of leafmould, 2 of sand and a quart of bonemeal added to each barrow-load of this mix. The pots must be well drained and when plants are grown indoors they should be left alone. Too much moving about, poor light or overwatering all cause leafdrop. Plenty of light is necessary to maintain and bring out the leaf colouring.

For propagation purposes, take a tall plant with a naked stem, cut it down to within 10cm (4in) of the soil, then cut the stem into 5cm (2in) pieces. Plant these in sandy soil and cover them with 2cm ($\frac{1}{2}$in) of the same mixture. Place the cuttings in a warm propagating frame with bottom heat of about 21c (70F) and keep the soil just moist. Eventually each cutting will send up a shoot and emit roots, after which it can be carefully potted and again kept warm until it starts to grow again.

In the Polynesian Islands the leaves of *Cordyline terminalis* are commonly used for wrapping around fish before baking. The leaf fibres are made into fringed skirts, and aboriginal Hawaiians made a fermented drink from the roots.

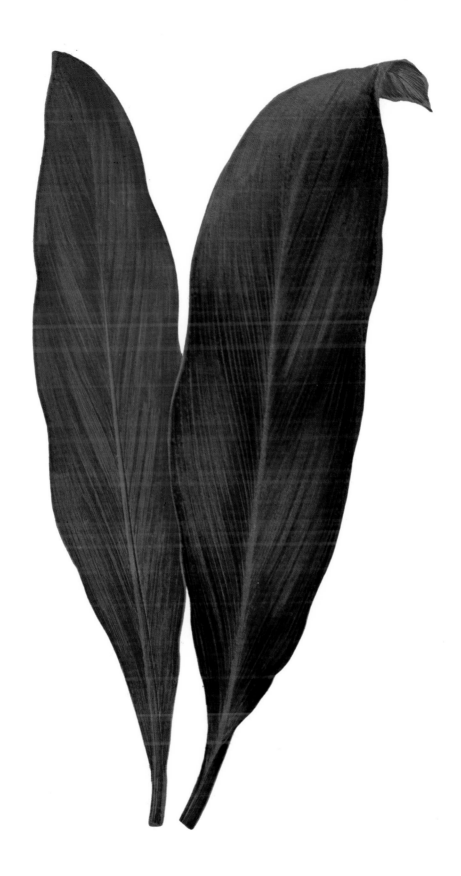

Daphne mezereum 'Variegatum'

MEZEREON

This is a rare variegated form of the mezereon, one of the finest and most easily cultivated daphnes. It blooms before the leaves appear, in late winter and early spring, its spicily fragrant, stalkless, four-lobed calyx (there are no petals) in dense clusters and varying in colour from pale lilac to ruby-red. There are also white varieties with single and double flowers. Daphnes belong to the natural order Thymelaeaceae and the species *Daphne mezereum* is a native of Europe, Siberia and western Asia. The variegated form portrayed appeared in 1856 in a batch of seedlings, raised by a Mr Joshua Major, a landscape gardener of Leeds. For some time it was perpetuated by grafting slips on to the type species, but it is doubtful if many – if any – specimens of this attractive plant remain in cultivation.

The mezereon is a small, rounded, many-branched deciduous shrub of 1–1.5m (3–5ft), with oblong or elliptic-lanceolate leaves 4–8cm (1½–3in) by 1–2cm (½–¾in) wide. It fruits freely, producing quantities of round, bright scarlet berries which are greedily taken by goldfinches. These provide the best means of increase and self-set seedlings are common around mature plants. Failing this, seed should be sown in seed compost (see Introduction, p. x). Half-ripe summer cuttings frequently root in sand and peat.

Daphne mezereum will grow in sun or light shade and in most garden soils, including chalk, provided the drainage is good.

The species seems to thrive – like Madonna lilies – in cottage gardens, but wherever they grow, plants apparently in good health and of mature size, may suddenly die for no discernible reason.

The whole plant – but particularly the fruit – is poisonous; I was once in agony for several hours after sampling a berry. Although birds take them freely, Linnaeus, the Swedish botanist, said that six berries would kill a wolf and that a girl he knew died after taking twelve to 'cure an ague'.

Before cosmetics were readily available Russian women would use the berries to bring a rosy hue to their cheeks, and artists also used them to produce a 'fine lake colour'. The dried root was at one time a popular specific for toothache.

Dichorisandra musaica

MOSAIC-LEAVED DICHORISANDRA

This handsome plant, which is valued equally for its flowers and foliage, belongs to the natural order Commelinaceae. An herbaceous perennial native to Brazil, it has terminal bunches of bright azure-blue, three-petalled flowers on 46cm (18in) stems. These appear in late summer but from spring until autumn one can enjoy the ovate-oblong, sharp-pointed, dark green leaves with their zig-zag white lines and veins on the upper surface, and their reddish-purple undersides.

Another species, *D.albo-marginata* (also known as *Campelia zanonia* or Mexican flag) grows taller, (60cm–1m (2–3ft)) and has blue petals with white bases, while the 1.2m (4ft) *D.thyrsiflora* – a fine winter-flowering plant for a warm room – has rich, dark-blue flowers with bright golden stamens. These are borne in compact trusses and there is also a variegated-leaved form of this species.

All the dichorisandras are native to tropical South America and will not tolerate cold conditions. Grow them in a warm greenhouse or centrally-heated room where temperatures do not drop below 14–15c (58–60f) in winter. They must be shaded from direct sunlight which bleaches the foliage, and also protected from draughts. A moist atmosphere is desirable, such as derives from standing the pots on pebbles in a tray which has a little water at the base. Water freely during the summer months, and feed the plants monthly with a soluble fertilizer during the growing season. In winter reduce the amount of water to a level just enough to keep the soil barely damp. Dichorisandras can be grown in a proprietary loamless compost or a made-up mixture composed of equal parts by bulk of coarse sand, leaf soil and loam.

The quickest method of propagation is by division of the roots in spring, but they may also be increased from seed sown in good heat (24c, 75f).

Dioscorea vittata 'Argyraea'

STRIPED YAM

This plant belongs to a genus of approximately 600 tropical and subtropical herbaceous twining plants, in the natural order Dioscoreaceae. Most have handsome, heart-shaped – occasionally lobed – leaves and, frequently, large edible tubers. The species *Dioscorea vittata*, also known as *Dioscorea discolor*, came to Europe from Colombia around 1820 as a stove-greenhouse plant. The cultivar 'Argyraea' has green leaves with lighter green patches and areas of silver around the midribs. The undersides are purplish-crimson and the usual size is 13cm (5in) wide and about 18cm (7in) long. These many-hued leaves show to greatest advantage when trained around a balloon-shaped framework of wires or canes.

The species is tuberous-rooted with inconspicuous green flowers.

Grow the plants in a light rich sandy soil, composed of equal parts by bulk of sandy peat, fibrous loam and leafmould with plenty of coarse river sand mixed throughout. Potting should take place in early spring as new growth starts. Provide plenty of water during the growing season but reduce the amount in autumn so as to keep the soil barely moist in winter. Temperatures around 15–18c (60–65f) are ideal.

Propagation is by division of the tubers – which form eyes like potatoes – during their resting period, *never* when they are growing.

A number of important economic plants belong to the genus. Yams are widely grown in wet tropical areas for their nutritious, starchy tubers. The Chinese yam, *Dioscorea batatas*, is not only cultivated as a food crop but an arrowroot is derived from the starch. The negro yam, *Dioscorea cayennensis*, bears edible roots weighing from 2–20kg (4–85lb) which are black with yellow flesh. These take a year to mature so the species is sometimes known as the twelve-month yam. *Dioscorea trifida*, the yampi, contains sapogenins used in the manufacture of cortisone. Dozens more have edible tubers, although these are rarely – if ever – exported.

Another species, *Dioscorea bulbifera*, is called the air potato because aerial tubers – sometimes weighing several pounds – are produced in the leaf axils. These are palatable and taste like potatoes, but the plant has no root tubers, or at most only very small ones.

Euonymus japonicus 'Aureopictus'

JAPANESE SPINDLE

Also known as the golden-striped Japanese spindle, *Euonymus japonicus* 'Aureopictus' (Syn. 'Aureus') is a low-growing evergreen shrub of up to 3m (10ft), ideal for coastal or town planting. It belongs to the natural order Celastraceae whose 176 species include *Euonymus europaeus*, the spindle tree of English copses and hedgerows. The variegated plant depicted here is less hardy than the green-leaved Japanese species, *E. japonicus*, so in exposed northerly situations give it a sheltered position, for example at the front of a shrubbery or against a wall. The leaves are ovate, 2–6cm ($\frac{3}{4}$–2$\frac{1}{4}$in) long and 2–4cm ($\frac{3}{4}$–1$\frac{1}{2}$in) wide, almost wholly yellow but banded with rich green margins. Although the flowers are insignificant, the habit is bushy and the leaf colouring so bright that a well-grown specimen can be really beautiful.

A light, well-drained soil suits the plant best. It does not object to chalk but dislikes wet low-lying ground.

Propagation may be effected by means of cuttings or layers. June is the best time for layering when the best variegated shoots should be carefully pulled down to soil level. Make a slit on the underside of these, a few inches down from the tip, peg the shoots down and cover the wounded part with an inch of sandy soil. By autumn they should have rooted and they can then be carefully separated from the parent plant and potted. Keep them under cover the first winter and plant them in their permanent positions the following spring.

Cuttings should be taken from a plant that has been kept under glass. It will have softer shoots and these will root more rapidly than those from outdoor specimens with tougher skins. Make the cuttings in spring and insert them in a sand and peat mixture in a warm propagating frame. Pot the plants separately when rooted and harden them off as recommended for layers. The variegated euonymus can also be grafted on the species – *Euonymus japonicus* – which incidentally makes a good evergreen hedge. Cattle thrive on its clippings although the foliage is sometimes attacked and can be riddled by caterpillars of the lesser ermine moth. To combat the latter use derris dust on the foliage as soon as the trouble is spotted.

Euphorbia pulcherrima

POINSETTIA

This well-known pot-plant comes from Mexico, where it was discovered by Dr. J. R. Poinsett in 1828 who brought it to Europe in 1834. Originally named *Poinsettia pulcherrima* after its finder, botanists later reclassified the plant and referred it to the genus Euphorbia, in the family Euphorbiaceae. Dr. Poinsett however is still remembered in its popular name – poinsettia.

The species is a long-lasting evergreen shrub (up to 3m (10ft) in the wild) with oval or lanceolate, incised leaves which bear some resemblance to oak leaves. The green leafy stems are topped by rosettes of flowering scarlet bracts, which spread like stars and are sometimes 30cm (12in) across. These presumably attract insects for pollination purposes, since the greenish-yellow flowers they surround are rather small and insignificant. Forms with pink and white bracts are also available.

At one time poinsettias were mainly raised for the Christmas market, but nowadays new growing techniques enable flowers (and bracts) to be produced at any season. Commonly referred to as 'short day' treatment, the method denies plants more than ten hours of light daily for eight successive weeks. The sustained periods of darkness are critical, for if these are broken – even by lamplight, the plants fail to set beds or to produce colourful bracts. Another modern technique is to water the soil or spray young plants with chemical dwarfing compounds, so that although they produce large flower-heads the stems remain short, 30–60cm (1–2ft) tall.

Poinsettias are not hardy and in winter require a day temperature around 18c (65F), with a drop of about 3c (5F) at night. Overwatering induces leafdrop and is the commonest cause of failure, so wait until the foliage droops slightly before giving the plants further liquid, using this at room temperature. After flowering, cut the shoots back to about 15cm (6in) and rest the plants (by giving them very little water) until autumn, when they can be watered more freely and restarted into growth.

Propagation is by means of cuttings, taken in spring where the shoots are 7–10cm (3–4in) long. Dip the cut ends of these in powdered charcoal to stop the white milky latex bleeding – and avoid getting it in cuts or wounds or it will cause intense irritation. Root the cuttings in a warm propagating case.

Fittonia verschaffeltii

SILVER-NERVE FITTONIA

Fittonias take their name from Elizabeth and Sarah Mary Fitton, joint authors of a book called *Conversations on Botany*, written in 1817. There are two species in the genus – both ornamental-leaved perennials belonging to the natural order Acanthaceae.

The plant illustrated has various synonyms – *Gymnostachyum verschaffeltii*, *Eranthemum verschaffeltii* and *Gymnostachyum bracteosum*. It is a creeping ground-cover plant with opposite oval leaves 7–10cm (2¾–4in) long and 5–7.5cm (2–3in) wide on short stalks. The insignificant pale-yellow flowers peep between green bracts on slender spikes, while the dark-green leaves are netted with deep red in the type species. This colouration is even more brilliant in the cultivar 'Pearcei'. Another splendid plant is the silver-veined 'Argyroneura', a popular kind for humid conditions and frequently used in bottle gardens.

Fittonias also make good carpeting plants underneath greenhouse staging but must be kept away from draughts and direct sunlight – although reasonably good light is essential to maintain the leaf colouring. Water with tepid, lime-free water and feed the plants when necessary with a weak nutrient solution used at half the strength recommended for ordinary house plants. They need careful handling as the stems are very brittle and do best in shallow, well-crocked pans or bowls of light, fibrous but humus-rich soil. They may also be grown in a proprietary loamless compost.

Reproduction is by means of soft cuttings which strike very easily in the moist heat, 18–21c (65–70f), of a propagating frame.

Graptophyllum pictum

CARICATURE PLANT

Graptophyllum pictum, which is also known as *Justicia picta* and *Graptophyllum hortense*, belongs to the natural order Acanthaceae. Its generic name is derived from the Greek *graptos*, to paint or write and *phyllon*, a leaf, an allusion to its curiously-marked leaves which bear some resemblance to faces. For this reason *Graptophyllum pictum* is often known as the caricature plant. Incidentally none of the leaves is exactly like another.

There are about ten species in the genus, all evergreen shrubs native to Australia, West Africa and the Pacific Islands. The species portrayed was introduced about 1780 and grows 2.5–3m (8–10ft) high. It has smooth green leaves, irregularly-marked with pale yellow along the midribs, elliptic in shape and arranged in pairs on creamy-yellow stems. In order to bring out the full variegation the plants should be exposed to full sunlight. The crimson flowers, borne in whorls in the leaf axils, are tubular with gaping, slightly hairy throats.

The caricature plant is not hardy and demands warmth at all times. Temperatures around 18–21c (65–70f) are appropriate in summer but should not drop below 10c (50f) in winter. Equal parts of fibrous loam, sand and peat with a half part of decayed animal-manure is the recommended compost, but they do just as well in a mixture of leafmould, peat and loam in equal proportions, plus a light sprinkling of sharp sand. Since the plants are apt to grow straggly, frequent stopping and pruning is necessary in order to induce a bushy habit.

Propagation by soft cuttings can take place in early spring, when the young shoots root readily in a mixture of peat and sand in a closed propagating frame with a bottom heat of 21c (70f). Later they can be potted separately and kept in a very light place to prevent the stems from becoming drawn.

Another species, *Graptophyllum earlii*, a tall shrub of 3–5m (10–16ft), comes from Queensland and is often grown in tropical gardens (or as a pot plant elsewhere) for its smooth, shiny, oblong leaves. The flowers are a rich red, either solitary or several together in the leaf axils.

Gravesia guttata

BERTOLONIA

Also known as *Bertolonia guttata*, this is one of some hundred Madagascan plants belonging to the natural order Melastomataceae. All are of dwarf habit with striking foliage and all require a moist atmosphere, with growing temperatures around 22–25c (72–78f) and light shade. These conditions are difficult to provide indoors so they are not easy plants to grow without a greenhouse. Fluctuating temperatures and draughts cause the leaves to collapse, but good prospects of success can be obtained if they are planted in a bottle garden or in a glass-sided terrarium with a covered top.

The soil should be light but rich, and only soft water should be applied. During the winter months *Gravesia guttata* may be rested, when it can withstand lower temperatures – around 14c (58f).

The plant has a long creeping root, as thick as a goose-quill, which bears some resemblance to a fern caudex. The leaves occur in pairs and are ovate and membranous 7.5–15cm (3–6in) long and 5–7.5cm (2–3in) wide, dark green with fine parallel veins, on either side of which are quantities of rosy spots. The younger leaves are a delicate cinnamon-brown while the under-surfaces of all the leaves are brownish-purple. The five-petalled flowers are produced at the summit of the plant, in an erect cyme carrying five to ten rosy-pink blossoms. There are various cultivars including 'Legrelleana' which has its veins outlined with white but no rosy spots; 'Superba', thickly spotted with reddish-purple, and 'Alfred Bleu' which has bright red veins and brilliant red spots.

Except for the cultivars which must be propagated by division, reproduction is easy from seeds sown in light compost and germinated in a warm propagating frame.

Hedera helix - Variegated Varieties

VARIEGATED IVIES

Hedera helix, the common ivy, is a European plant belonging to the natural order Araliaceae. A hardy evergreen climber, it romps up high walls and buildings, clinging to rough surfaces by means of aerial sucker-like roots, a circumstance noted in its specific name *helix*, which is Latin for a screw or nail and refers to the way it twines itself around supports. When it reaches the summit of its climb, then – and only then – does it produce flowers and fruits: the former small and yellowish-green in rounded umbels, the latter small black berries which appear around Christmas time.

Ivies are useful for masking ugly buildings or bleak north walls, although they should not be allowed to get under house tiles or in gutters. They also make good ground-cover beneath trees and in similar shady places and they are very popular for this purpose in the United States. Additionally they make good pot plants for cool rooms, either grown up stakes, allowed to droop over shelves as trailers, trained in various shapes around wire foundations, or made into small trees by careful pruning.

The variegated kinds are especially ornamental, with variously-shaped and sized leaves, which may be blotched, edged or suffused with gold, silver or rose. A representative selection is shown in the illustration.

Ivies in gardens are undemanding and suitable for most soils, but when grown as pot plants they are usually cultivated in a rich mixture, such as John Innes Compost or Rochford's special house-plant formula (see Introduction page x). Sometimes variegated ivies lose their colour and revert to green. When this occurs wait until spring and then cut the plant back to the first variegated leaf. It should then make new shoots with variegated leaves. Water moderately at all times, in winter giving the plants very little but keeping the leaves clean by an occasional sponging with clean water.

Propagation is by means of cuttings, rooted in equal parts by bulk of sand and peat. Keep them in a closed container to hasten rooting, which with certain varieties can take a long time. For pot work it is advisable to plant several rooted cuttings together in order to effect a quicker and better display.

Hibiscus rosa-sinensis 'Cooperi'

HIBISCUS

Also known as shoeflower or Chinese rose, hibiscus is native to southern China from whence it was introduced to Europe early in the eighteenth century. It belongs to the same natural order (Malvaceae) as the hollyhock, to which it bears some resemblance, and it is one of 300 species in the genus. Although it grows up to 4.5m (15ft) in tropical gardens, 2–2.5m (6–8ft) is a more general size for tub specimens, or less than 1m (3ft) when pruned back and kept in pots. The flowers are large, usually 12–15cm (5–6in) in diameter, with five petals of an intense scarlet with crimson bases, surrounding long protruding staminal columns bearing many short pollen-daubed filaments. Cultivars with semi-double or double flowers exist, and various other colours – yellow, orange, red and pink – besides the fine foliage form of our illustration known as 'Cooperi'. This is a shy bloomer but it has rainbow foliage of vivid green, heavily splashed and blotched with dark green, creamy-white, pink and crimson. Its leaves are lanceolate or elongate-ovate, wedge-shaped at the base, pointed at the tip and toothed at the edges. Being less hardy than the species, it is best kept indoors or in a greenhouse throughout the year.

Cultivation in pots is not difficult provided the plants are kept in a good light. A compost of equal parts by bulk of fibrous loam and lumpy peat, with enough sand to make the mix porous, suits them well, or they can be grown in John Innes No. 2 Potting Compost. Hibiscus plants need plenty of water in summer for if the soil dries out the buds will drop. In early autumn decrease the quantity so as to keep the soil barely moist all winter. Pruning takes place in late winter, when the branches can be shortened – drastically if necessary. Propagation is by means of soft-tip cuttings, taken in early summer and rooted in a warm propagating frame, soil temperature 24–26c (75–80F).

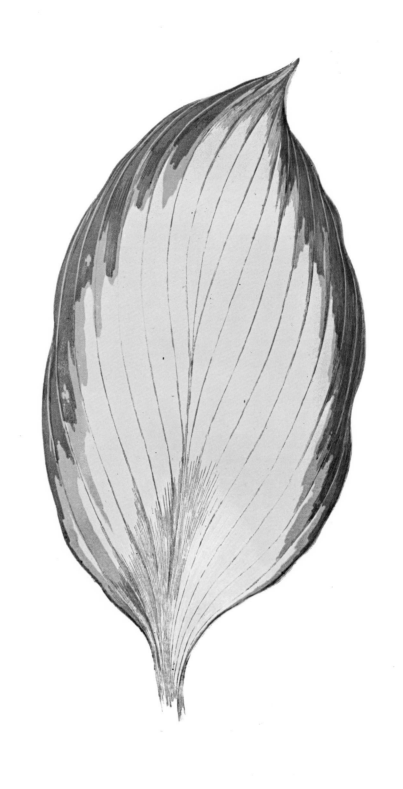

Hosta fortunei 'Albopicta'

PLANTAIN LILY

Hostas comprise a genus of some twenty or so species, all from China and Japan and belonging to the natural order Liliaceae. They are hardy herbaceous perennials, known also as funkias or plantain lilies, and they thrive best in damp fertile soil, in partial or even full shade. In full sun they produce more flowers but are prone to suffer from drought, unless the roots are constantly kept moist. Sun also bleaches the foliage. An occasional mulch of rotted leaves benefits established plants and is particularly important on thin chalk soils.

Plantain lilies are mainly cultivated for their foliage which has a statuesque quality and is very varied; the Japanese species *Hosta fortunei* and its cultivars are among the most dependable and spectacular. The form 'Albopicta' grows 45–60cm (18–24in) tall, with long-stalked, broadly ovate leaves of bright yellow edged with pale green. These are 20–25cm (8–10in) long and 8–10cm (3–4in) wide. As summer advances the green darkens and the yellow fades to primrose. Spikes of nodding, lilac, trumpet-shaped flowers, each about 4cm (1½in) long are produced in mid-summer on smooth 60–75cm (2–2½ft) stems. These are good for cutting.

'Aurea' has all-yellow leaves when young, gradually fading to green. There is a cultivar with white leaf edges called 'Marginato-Alba' and another with yellow margins to its green leaves called 'Obscura Marginata'.

Hostas are ideal plants for the edges of shady woodlands, although leafdrip sometimes disfigures the foliage. They are also splendid plants for the vicinity of water gardens and make good container specimens when planted in humus-rich soil.

Plants are easily propagated by division at practically any season, but preferably in spring and autumn. Lift and split the clumps into sections, or detach small side-shoots from a mature specimen. When happily situated the plants grow rapidly to bold clumps, although protection from slugs and snails may be necessary in early summer to safeguard the young foliage.

Hoya carnosa 'Variegata'

VARIEGATED WAXFLOWER

Also known as *Asclepias carnosa*, *Hoya carnosa* belongs to the natural order Asclepiadaceae. It is an evergreen climber from Australia, introduced to Europe about 1802. At one time it was widely grown in greenhouses and conservatories as a button-hole plant, the pinkish-white flowers, in short-stalked drooping umbels of twelve to fifteen blossoms, having a waxy texture which enabled them to last a long time without water. Unfortunately they also secrete nectar which makes them sticky to touch.

The 8cm by 4cm (3in by 1½in) leaves are oval-oblong in shape, slender-pointed with a thick fleshy texture. They grow alternately along the twining 2m (6–8ft) stems and are deep green in the species but richly variegated with pale pink and cream in *Hoya carnosa* 'Variegata'.

Hoyas must be kept indoors in cool climates, in a light position but away from direct sunlight and draughts. Too much winter warmth causes lanky stems, badly developed foliage and attacks from greenfly, so aim at winter temperatures of 10–12c (50–54f). This can be stepped up gradually to 15–18c (60–65f) in spring to encourage rapid growth. For pot work the stems should be trained around wire frames or canes to keep them of manageable size.

Indifferent watering is the commonest cause of failure with hoyas. Give plenty during the growing period, then gradually decrease the amount until from autumn onwards (when they are moved to a cooler position) they only receive sufficient water to keep the soil from drying out. Later, following transference to summer quarters, the supply can be gradually increased.

The variegated waxflower does not need rich soil; a suitable compost consists of equal parts by bulk of loam, peat and small pieces of crocks or bricks mixed with old lime rubble. Older plants should not be repotted too often as this affects the variegation, but when it becomes essential repot in early spring.

Propagation is effected by taking young pieces of shoot and rooting these as cuttings in a propagator with bottom heat.

Hydrangea x macrophylla 'Quadricolor'

VARIEGATED HYDRANGEA

The genus Hydrangea consists of deciduous and evergreen shrubs, climbers and small trees from North America, East Asia, and the Philippines. In gardens they are chiefly represented by cultivars derived from several Japanese species, notably *H. macrophylla* and *H. serrata*, which are collectively grouped as *Hydrangea × macrophylla*. These are all deciduous, the leaves ovate with serrated edges.

This group is again subdivided into hortensias and lacecaps. Hortensias are large, mop-headed, sterile flower types used in pot culture and grown extensively in gardens. Lacecaps have flattish blooms composed almost entirely of fertile flowers, surrounded by a ring of the more showy sterile florets. It is to this group that the cultivar 'Quadricolor' belongs.

Lacecaps require cooler conditions than hortensias, and do better in acid soils. For this reason they are most at home in a woodland setting, associating particularly well with rhododendrons, camellias, lilies and azaleas. The cream, green and grey variegations of 'Quadricolor' look well against dark foliage, but since the plant only grows about 1m 22cm (4ft) high it should be given a forward position in mixed borders. The flowers are pale pink or blue according to the nature of the soil, but if the plant is liberally dressed with peat and watered occasionally with a sequestrene compound or aluminium sulphate the blue tends to predominate.

Prune in spring, removing weak and frost-damaged branches, letting in light and air to the remainder. Propagation is carried out by means of cuttings, taken in midsummer from strong shoots of the current season's growth and rooted separately in 8cm (3in) pots of sand, loam and peat in equal proportions. Keep them in a close atmosphere until rooted and plant outside the following spring or autumn.

There are some eighty species of hydrangea, a few with slight economic uses. In Japan the dried leaves of *H. thunbergii* are used to make tea, and the bark and fine-grained wood of *H. paniculata* for paper, walking-sticks and pipes. In the eastern United States hydrangin is extracted from the roots of *H. arborescens* and used medicinally as a diuretic.

Ligularia tussilaginea 'Aureo-maculata'

LEOPARD PLANT

Ligularias are plants with daisy-type flowers belonging to the giant family of Compositae. The genus comprises some 150 species, all from temperate regions of Europe and Asia. *Ligularia tussilaginea*, also known as *Farfugium grande* and *Senecio kaempferi*, comes from Japan and is a herbaceous perennial with a rhizomatous rootstock and large, long-stalked, round or kidney-shaped leaves, 15–25cm (6–10in) across on 30cm (12in) stems. *Ligularia tussilaginea* 'Aureo – maculata', the form portrayed, has its dark green leaves blotched with yellow, white, and – occasionally – pink spots.

Given a sheltered site it is hardy in areas where it is unlikely to experience severe winters. Elsewhere it should be grown in soil borders in a greenhouse or used as a pot plant indoors. A good light is essential, but avoid a position where sun shining through glass falls directly on the leaves; otherwise they will burn or collapse. In a mixed collection the plant is distinct and striking, making a dense bushy specimen 1m–1.3m (3–4ft) across. The light-yellow flowers, each 2–5cm (1–2in) across, appear in late summer on branched 30–60cm (1–2ft) woolly stems.

Ligularias do well in loamless composts (see Introduction, page x) or in a mixture of equal parts by bulk of heavy fibrous loam, leafmould, sand and peat. Plenty of water is required during the growing season, also a monthly feed of liquid manure. Repotting should take place in early spring.

Propagation is mainly by division, from side-shoots attached to the main plant. These can be separated, with some roots attached, potted on separately and kept in a shaded frame or propagating case for a few days, after which they may be hardened off under cooler conditions and kept in a light place, such as a north window.

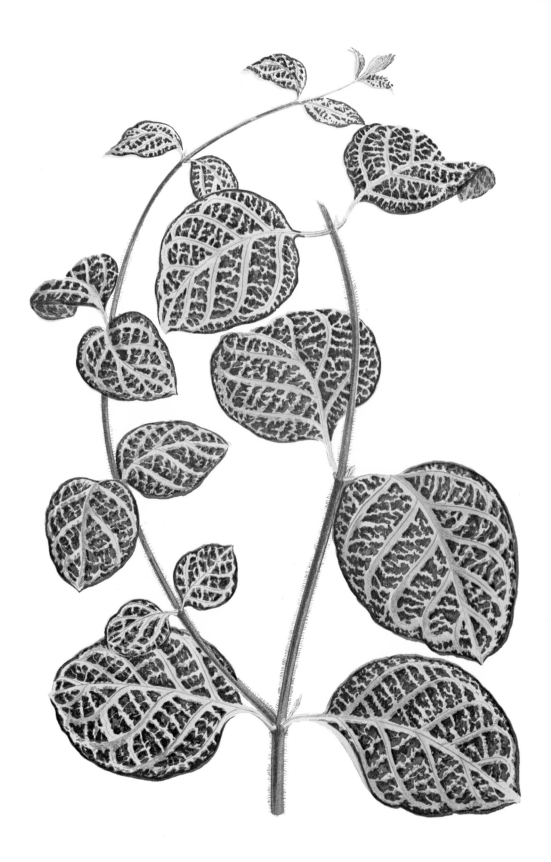

Lonicera japonica 'Aureo-reticulata'

JAPANESE HONEYSUCKLE

Loniceras belong to the natural order Caprifoliaceae, a genus comprising about 180 deciduous and evergreen bushy or climbing shrubs. They take their generic name from Adam Lonitzer (1528–86), a German botanist.

The specimen portrayed is a hardy, variegated-leaved climbing honeysuckle, one of the many acquisitions brought back from Japan by Robert Fortune in the middle of the nineteenth century. It is an evergreen of vigorous habit, although inclined to be less hardy than its green-foliaged parent *Lonicera japonica*. The leaves are less than 5cm (2in) long and variable in shape, mostly ovate but sometimes pinnately lobed so that they bear some resemblance to oak leaves, particularly when young. The veins and midribs of 'Aureo-reticulata' are picked out and netted with fine golden lines, mottled in summer with pink. This gives the plant a glowing sunshiny look that has special appeal in a shady situation. To obtain flowers however it is necessary to give it a sunny wall or trellis and to refrain from pruning except to prevent overcrowding. In due course the mature wood will then produce pairs of fragrant white and yellow flowers in the leaf axils.

The cultivar can also be grown in a large container, provided it has wire or trellis up which to clamber. Any light soil of reasonable quality is suitable. Alternatively, container specimens can be grown in John Innes No. 2 Potting Compost. Cool root conditions should be maintained.

Propagation is effected by means of cuttings, using firm young shoots of the current season's growth. These should be cut across just under a joint and rooted in gentle bottom heat in late summer. Alternatively cuttings of riper wood can be taken in early autumn and rooted in sandy soil in a cold frame, or under a cloche, outdoors.

Musa x paradisiaca 'Vittata'

ORNAMENTAL BANANA

This handsome, variegated-leaved form of the edible banana makes a striking addition to any collection of foliage subjects, although it needs plenty of room to develop. It is an admirable plant for a light, centrally-heated hall, a warm greenhouse or a large well-lit room, particularly when it can be displayed as a centrepiece surrounded by other plants.

The genus *Musa* belongs to the natural order Musaceae and was named in honour of Antonius Musa, physician to the Emperor Octavius Augustus (63–14BC). In southern Asia the use of bananas for food is believed to stem back to prehistoric times. Ancient Greek and Roman writers refer to the plant as 'a remarkable Indian tree' and certainly it figures frequently in early Buddhist art and is described in the Koran as the 'paradise tree'

The variegated-leaved form has been known in northern Europe since the beginning of the nineteenth century when it was occasionally grown in warm conservatories and greenhouses. It can be planted in a large pot or tub in rich soil, composed of good turfy loam, with well-rotted manure at the base of the container. Plenty of water is required throughout the growing period and temperatures should not fall below 13–15C (55–60F).

Although *Musa* × *paradisiaca* 'Vittata' can grow 6m (20ft) under ideal conditions, and even bear small clusters of fruit, approximately half that height is more usual when the roots are confined. The large, bright green, spirally-arranged leaves are heavily splashed with white; they are oblong in shape, with bold midribs and parallel veins. Stems which bear fruit die later and are replaced by suckers springing up from the base. These can be detached and potted for propagating purposes.

Passiflora trifasciata

PASSION FLOWER

There is a legend that when the first Spanish priests followed the Conquistadores into South America, they looked for a sign that Catholicism would become the religion of this new land. Almost immediately they found a passion flower growing near the sea-shore. They compared its ten outer petals to the Apostles (omitting Simon Peter and the doubting Thomas), the countless blue filaments inside each bloom to the many disciples, the five stamens to the five wounds of Christ, and the three-parted stigma to the Holy Trinity. Additionally the plant provided food – the fruits of some species, like the granadilla (*P. quadrangularis*) being edible – and so the passion flower became the plant of hope and promise.

P. trifasciata comes from Peru, in the natural order Passifloraceae. It is noteworthy for its attractive leaves, which are up to 12cm (5in) long and 10cm (4in) wide and three-parted, the central lobe being the largest. When young these present a pleasing combination of grassy-green overlaid along the course of the principal veins, with three irregular bands of mottled grey and pale green. These colours coalesce near the leaf-stalks. As the leaves mature the grey changes to rose and then to deep red or even scarlet and, at a later stage of growth, to purple, brown or maroon. Finally, when the leaves start to decay these colours fade in the reverse order of appearance until at last they are practically white.

The species is a robust climber and in addition to its colourful leaves produces 2.5–4cm (1½in), very fragrant, yellowish-white flowers. It will grow in any good compost in a greenhouse border or a large container, and benefits from monthly feeds with a liquid fertilizer during the summer months. Give plenty of water at this time but very little in winter. The plant appreciates warmth and sunshine, and temperatures should never fall below 10c (50f) at any time of year. It is also necessary to provide the plant with supports up which it may climb. To propagate, make cuttings in spring of young pieces of shoot, preferably with a heel, and root these in a warm propagating frame.

Pelargoniums

TRICOLOR-LEAVED GERANIUMS

Pelargoniums are well-known, brilliant and long-flowering plants widely grown as pot plants and for summer bedding. The genus, with 250 species almost exclusively South African, belongs to the natural order Geraniaceae. Commonly, but erroneously called geraniums – a name more correctly applicable to the cranesbills – zonal pelargoniums are mainly derived from crossings between *Pelargonium inquinans* and *P. zonale*. These have rounded green leaves, velvety to the touch, with scalloped edges and a dark horseshoe marking at the centre of each leaf. When bruised the foliage emits a singular 'geranium' scent. The single or double flowers are carried in round umbels on long leafless stems, and may be pink, white, orange, rose, scarlet or magenta. Many named cultivars have been raised – one firm in 1910 offered 800 varieties – dwarfs and miniatures as well as the normal 30–60cm (1–2ft) types. Plants of the normal-sized varieties, trained against a wall in a warm greenhouse, often grow to 2m (6ft) in a couple of years. 'Madame Salleroi', a small-leaved variety with white-margined leaves, is a favourite for edging purposes. Occasionally it throws shoots with the colouring reversed. This form has been separately classified as a distinct variety, called 'Mrs Newton' or 'Little Trot'.

The plants in our illustration are all varieties over a hundred years old and it is doubtful whether any are still in existence. However, near counterparts can be found in most modern collections, the tricolour 'Mr Henry Cox', with yellow, green and red leaves being one of the best.

Pelargoniums need plenty of light and are easily propagated from cuttings taken in spring or late summer and rooted in sandy compost. Later they should be potted in a good potting compost like John Innes No. 2 and fed occasionally when in flower. Water if necessary, but not too much, as this encourages leaves rather than flowers and also detracts from the brightness of their colouring. They should be lifted before frost occurs, if grown outside, and stored for winter in a greenhouse – temperature 6–8c (43–46f) – until spring.

Peperomia argyreia

SILVER PEPEROMIA

Peperomias belong to the natural order Peperomiaceae and are native to the tropical rain forests of South America. This indicates their liking for moist, humid conditions, so not surprisingly most of the species make good plants for carboy gardens and similar closed containers. But they can also be cultivated as house plants, either in mixed communities with other plants or grown separately in small pots. To maintain sufficient humidity indoors it is usual to stand them on pebbles in a bowl or tray which always has a little water in the base.

There are green-leaved species, creeping species, and species with variegated foliage. *Peperomia argyreia*, which is also known as *P. sandersii*, comes in the last category and has succulent, orbicular ovate leaves which look like small fleshy shields. These have the veins radiating outwards from the centre like the spokes of an umbrella, bright green along the nerves but silvery between them. The stems are red and the leaves 8–12cm (3¼–4¾in) long. The plant grows compactly, 20–23cm (8–9in) high, the minute petal-less flowers being borne on long spikes. It will retain its attractive appearance throughout the year provided it is protected from draughts and strong sunlight and not allowed to get too wet or too dry. Temperatures should not drop below 10c (50F) at any time. Use soft water for watering and feed it monthly with a liquid fertilizer during the summer. The potting soil should be light but contain plenty of humus, such as a loamless compost or a mix made up from equal parts by bulk of coarse sand and leaf soil with a little decayed cow-manure if possible. Porous clay pots are preferable to plastic pots.

Propagation of *P. argyreia* is by cutting the leaves into two or four segments and inserting the cut ends of these in sand and peat (equal parts) in a warm (21c, 70F) propagating case. Baby plants will then be produced at the base of each vein and can be detached and potted on.

Phalaenopsis schilleriana

MOTH ORCHID

Phalaenopsis schilleriana is charming when in flower but attractive through-
out the year for the exquisite marbling of its young foliage. The species, one
of 35 in the genus, belongs to the natural order Orchidaceae. It is native to the
Philippines, and it was introduced into Europe by the German Consul
Schiller of Hamburg and given his name by the celebrated botanist Professor
Reichenbach.

The plant is an epiphyte and in its native haunts grows on lofty branches
and tree trunks in the dryer parts of the forests, never in damp localities. It
should not be kept too wet or too warm.

The oblong, blunt-ended, fleshy leaves grow from 15–45cm (6–18in) long.
They are dark green above with grey or whitish suffusions, and purple underneath. The blooms appear in winter and early spring, when the foliage may
lose some of its mottled lustre, but the flowers compensate for this. They are
mostly white but with yellow markings towards the centres and some rosy-
lilac spotting. The depth of these colours varies, and so does the number of
flowers on each spike. Normally these hold twenty to thirty flowers but
instances have occurred where a hundred blooms have been found – all on one
drooping stem, one metre (3ft) in length.

This orchid should be grown in a teak basket with openwork sides or in a
suspended container with side perforations, using a compost composed of
osmunda fibre and sphagnum moss in equal parts, together with a few
decayed oak leaves. When this material becomes old and stale it should be
replaced. Keep the plants in a greenhouse, shaded from direct sunlight and
with a winter temperature around 21c (70f). In summer keep a buoyant
atmosphere by opening the top vents.

Water and syringe the plants freely in summer, using soft water, but do not
let moisture remain on the foliage all night. Water moderately in winter and
avoid draughts or sudden fluctuations in temperature. Propagation is difficult
as the species is slow to make offsets, although occasionally young plants
appear on the flower stems. These should be left to form their own roots before
being detached.

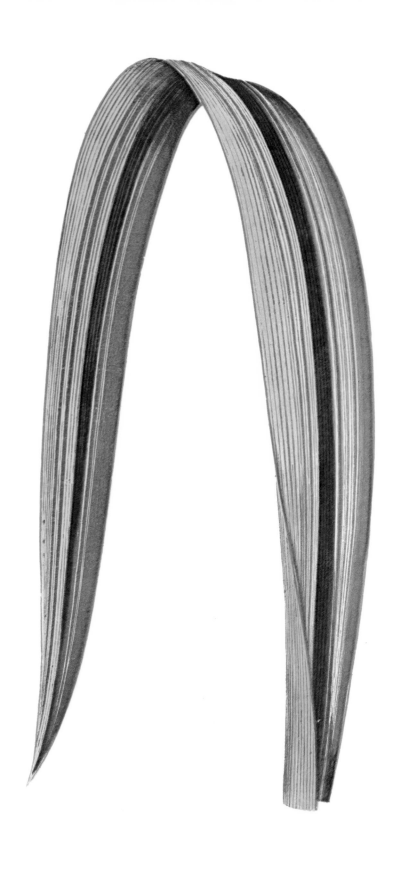

Phormium tenax 'Variegatum'

NEW ZEALAND FLAX

Phormiums are New Zealand evergreens belonging to the natural order Agavaceae. There are only two species: *Phormium tenax*, commonly known as New Zealand flax, which has strong, sword-shaped leaves up to 2.7m (9ft) long and about 5cm (2in) wide and the shorter-growing mountain flax, *P. colensoi* (*P. cookianum*).

P. tenax was discovered by Sir Joseph Banks and P. Solander when they accompanied Captain Cook on his first voyage round the world (1768–71). The thick and tough leaves produce a strong fibre which Maori maidens traditionally use for their fringed skirts, as well as for cordage, baskets, sacking and the like. Since the phormium is the only non-tropical fibre-producing plant, Sir Joseph Banks endeavoured to persuade growers to produce it commercially in Britain. Many experiments were carried out to test its qualities, both in Britain and France, but although the fibre grown in Europe proved to be quite as strong, although coarser, than that obtained from New Zealand, it was never produced in sufficient quantity to make it an economic proposition and the project failed.

The green-leaved *P. tenax* is well known as a conservatory plant, and in sheltered places like the south of Europe, southern England, western Scotland and southern Ireland it thrives well and even flowers outdoors. It is a plant of noble proportions, making imposing clumps, from the centres of which appear tall (3–5m; 9–16ft) flower spikes carrying many chocolate-brown flowers in midsummer.

The form figured here, var. 'Variegatum', is equally hardy and more impressive in garden settings. Its leaves are boldly marked with alternate stripings of green, amber and bright yellow – and occasionally red stripes as well.

All phormiums make good tub plants, an advantage in cold climates as they can be moved under cover in winter. Grow them in any good potting compost, in full sun, and water them freely in summer. Outdoors they can go in any good garden soil. Propagation is carried out by division of the clumps in spring or early autumn.

Pteris argyraea

STRIPED BRAKE

This beautiful East Indian pteris, belonging to the natural order Pteridaceae, made its appearance in 1858 via the famous nineteenth-century English nursery of James Veitch of Chelsea and became an immediate success with fern-loving Victorians.

It is of free growth and elegant habit, rising 1m (3ft) high and spreading its beautiful fronds in the most graceful manner. One of its common names, silver brake fern, is apt and descriptive, for the pinnae or side leaves of every frond have a broad central stripe of silvery, shining white down their centres, margined with light green. Although it was once designated as a form of *Pteris biaurita* botanists have now given the plant specific status.

Since it comes from the tropics the silver brake fern needs warm temperatures and humid growing conditions. It is best planted in well-crocked pots of sandy peat and leafmould, in equal proportions, mixed together with a few pieces of crushed charcoal. Lime is anathema to most ferns, so use soft water in those areas where the water is hard or contains calcium and other salts. If the pots are stood on a shingle tray with a little water in the base this promotes humidity around the undersides of the fronds. Keep the plant away from strong light and the fronds will be more distinctly striped. They need shade in order to develop good variegation.

Propagation is by means of division, which should be undertaken in spring. Wait until the plant has made several crowns, then remove one carefully without damaging its roots. Pot this in the soil mixture recommended and provide plenty of shade for a week or two to enable it to recover. After this gradually bring the plant into the normal light of the home or greenhouse.

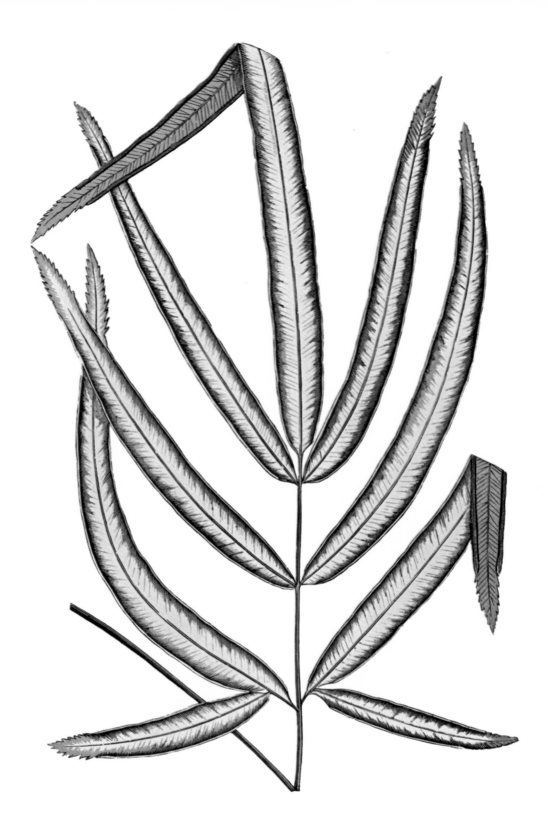

Pteris cretica 'Albolineata'

RIBBON FERN

Native to many temperate and tropical regions *Pteris cretica* is popularly known as the ribbon fern on account of the arrangement of its spores, which are borne in continuous bands along the lower leaf margins. It is a variable species with many cultivars and forms, some of which are variegated as in 'Albolineata', the plant portrayed here. The long green fronds of this plant have greenish-white central bands, each with three pairs of opposite pinnae and a terminal one, on a wiry 15–30cm (6–12in) stem. It makes a bushy plant, undemanding if kept moist. The fronds remain a very long time in good condition; in fact it is rarely necessary to remove a bad one.

Ribbon ferns should be kept under glass and provided with humid conditions for most of the year. They benefit from being stood outside occasionally in a warm summer shower. Keep them out of the sun at all times and to maintain humidity either stand the pots on a gravel tray (see Introduction, page xii) or plunge them in larger containers filled with damp peat moss. Temperatures around 15–18c (60–65F) are suitable. Water liberally during the growing season, using soft or lime-free water at room temperature. Decrease the amount in winter so as to keep the soil barely damp.

Ribbon ferns should be grown in well-crocked pots of the following soil mixture: 2 parts by bulk rough or turfy peat, 1 part lime-free loam and 1 part leafmould plus a liberal sprinkling of sharp sand, the whole thoroughly mixed.

New plants come true from spores although they take a long time to make sizeable specimens. Sow them on damp peat and sand in well-crocked pans, and place in a propagating case with a temperature around 25c (78F). As they grow the small ferns should be pricked out in tiny pots of similar soil mixture to the above, and potted on as necessary.

Rhapis excelsa

FAN PALM

Also known as *Rhapis flabelliformis*, this is one of the dwarf fan palms native to the Orient. *Rhapis excelsa* comes from China and Japan and makes a thumb-sized trunk about 46cm (18in) tall which is wrapped around by the persistent fibrous bases of old leaves. The last are borne alternately on slender stems, each of them deeply cut into five or seven, entire, spiny-edged segments. These are green in the species but delightfully striped with yellow in the form portrayed. This form, called by some authorities *foliis-variegatus* and by others *foliis luteo-vittata*, was introduced in 1861 by John Standish, an English nurseryman at Bagshot, Surrey, who was responsible for raising the wealth of Chinese and Japanese plants introduced by Robert Fortune between the years 1848 and 1860. The species, one of fifteen in this genus belongs to the natural order Palmae.

The plant needs very good drainage and must be grown in a well-crocked pot of rich loam with a little leafmould and sand, or alternatively in a made-up compost like John Innes Potting Compost No. 3. It requires plenty of water in summer but only enough to prevent drying out in winter. The variegated-leaved form is very slow-growing, needs full sunshine, and should be fed with a liquid fertilizer monthly during the growing season. It may be stood outside for the summer (the green form is almost hardy) and propagated by severing and potting the suckers or offshoots.

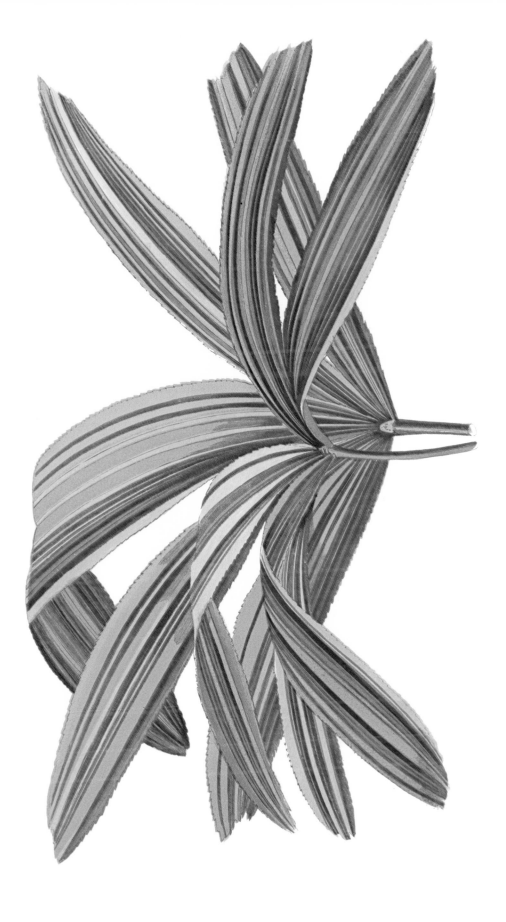

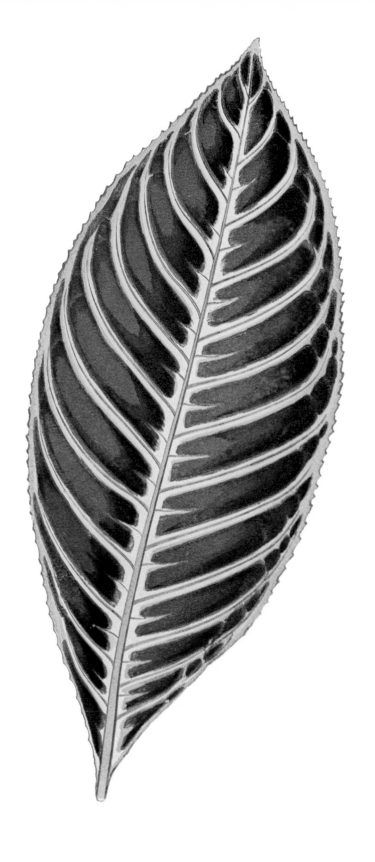

Sanchezia nobilis

NOBLE SANCHEZIA

Sanchezia nobilis comes from Ecuador and was introduced to Britain by the famous Victorian firm of nurserymen, Veitch and Son of Chelsea, in 1866. It is still grown as a house plant by those connoisseurs who are able to maintain a growing temperature which never falls below 10C (50F) in winter and will go considerably higher during the growing season. Normally this means keeping the plants in heated greenhouses or centrally-heated homes or offices. It belongs to the natural order Acanthaceae and in many respects resembles the better-known, yellow-flowered *Aphelandra squarrosa louisae*.

When well grown, *Sanchezia nobilis* makes a noble specimen of 30cm–1m (1–3ft). It is really a shrub, though it is usually grown as an herbaceous perennial in temperate climates. The four-sided stems are clothed with opposite, ovate-oblong, toothed and slender-pointed leaves each about 15–20cm (6–8in) in length. These are glaucous green with yellow stripes along the midribs and principal veins. The blooms come in midsummer, in terminal panicles consisting of eight to ten yellow flowers, each enclosed in a pair of large, bright red, concave bracts. Such combinations of colour in both flowers and leaves make for brilliant effects.

Sanchezia nobilis requires light but rich soil, or a good proprietary mix such as John Innes No. 2 Potting Compost, and it should also be fed regularly (at two-week intervals) during the growing season. Full exposure to sunshine is essential and warm temperatures, around 18c (65F) or over. The soil must never be allowed to dry out or the leaves will fall; on the other hand, it must never be too wet. A good compromise is to stand the pots in summer on a gravel tray which has a little water over the base. This will also give the plants the necessary humidity to prevent white fly and scale insect infestations on the foliage. In winter the pots can go on a dry bench and be watered just enough to keep the soil damp. Propagation is by cuttings of young wood taken during spring or early summer and rooted in sand and peat in a propagating frame with bottom heat. A temperature around 21–24c (70–75F) is necessary at this stage.

Saxifraga stolonifera 'Tricolor'

MOTHER OF THOUSANDS

Also known as *Saxifraga sarmentosa*, this beautiful leaved plant was introduced by Robert Fortune from Japan in 1863. There are about 370 species in the genus which belongs to the natural order Saxifragaceae, all northern temperate plants, chiefly alpine.

On arrival *Saxifraga stolonifera* quickly found favour with greenhouse enthusiasts and is still widely grown as a house plant, variously known – because of its rich colouring and habit of forming runners with small plantlets attached – as mother of thousands, Aaron's beard, roving sailor and strawberry geranium. The lobed and rounded, somewhat hairy and long-stalked leaves are handsomely marked with green, white and red blotches, the pink and red variegations being most obvious on the young foliage. The leaf-stalks are red.

The plant flowers in midsummer on 23–30cm (9–12in) stems. These occur in panicles, each bloom white with yellow speckles and small red spots on the inner petals, and two larger, drooping outer petals. To develop rich leaf colour it is necessary to keep the plants in small containers and in poor soil; too much nourishment induces greenness and rank growth.

The cultivar 'Tricolor' makes a delightful hanging-basket plant, with its leafy stolons and small plantlets trailing down all round the edges. The species is almost hardy, but must not be subjected to frost, nor should it be over-watered during the winter dormant period. 'Tricolor' needs still warmer conditions: approximately 10–15c (50–60f).

The best soil mix for container plants consists of equal parts by bulk of sand and peat with a half-part loam, or John Innes No. 1 Potting Compost. Propagation is carried out by removing little plantlets from the runners in early summer, and potting them up in groups of three.

Scindapsus pictus 'Argyraeus'

DEVIL'S IVY

Also known as *Pothos argyraea*, silver vine and devil's ivy, *Scindapsus pictus* 'Argyraeus' is the juvenile form of the Malayan species *Scindapsus pictus*. There are about forty species in the genus, which belongs to the natural order Araceae, the main areas of distribution being tropical Asia and the East Indies.

Devil's ivy is a strong evergreen climber, up to 12.5m (40ft) in its wild state, with warted, slender branches carrying 10–15cm (4–6in) long heart-shaped, sharp-pointed leaves. Arranged alternately on the stems, these are green with pale green spots on mature plants but delightfully flecked with white (instead of pale green) and only 5cm (2in) long when young. This juvenile form is the kind most commonly cultivated and has become a popular house plant for warm rooms. Only under ideal conditions, such as in a stove greenhouse, will the white arum-shaped, 5–8cm (2–3in) flowers be produced.

Scindapsus pictus 'Argyraeus' requires growing temperatures around 18–24c (65–75f), although it can survive short periods under cooler conditions. It seems impervious to gas and oil fumes and does particularly well where there is bottom heat, for example over a radiator (provided there is some form of insulation between radiator and pot) or on a TV set. An attractive way to grow it is round a cone of 2.5cm (1in) wire netting, inserted in the pot and stuffed with damp sphagnum moss. The plant will root into the moss and receive the moisture and humidity so necessary under central-heating conditions. It can also be grown strapped to a moss-covered tree trunk or on a block of tree fern root; or it can be grown as a basket plant, the shoots being pegged down and allowed to droop over the sides of the container. When grown indoors devil's ivy should be kept out of bright sunlight, otherwise the silvery blotches turn pale green.

Suitable planting composts include loamless compost (see Introduction page x) or equal parts of fibrous loam and half-decayed leaves mixed together with a few pieces of charcoal and enough sharp sand to keep the soil open. Give plenty of water in summer but only enough to keep the soil damp in winter.

Setaria palmifolia niveo-vittatum

VARIEGATED PALM GRASS

Also known as *Panicum palmifolium* and *P. plicatum* this handsome grass comes from the East Indies and belongs to the natural order Gramineae. There are about 140 species in the genus, some of them important fodder plants like the Italian millet (*S. italica*), which is cultivated as a cereal from southern Europe to Japan and has apparently been grown in China since 2700 BC. In the United States it is used as a hay crop.

The plant illustrated is the variegated form of *Setaria palmifolia* known as *niveo-vittatum* which was introduced by Messrs Veitch and Son in 1868. It is a robust but tender plant which must be grown in a greenhouse except during the height of summer, with 2.5–5cm (1–2in) wide, 1.2m (4ft) long flat grassy leaves of deep green with white stripes of various widths and occasionally red tinges along the margins. If it can be kept growing in sufficient warmth the foliage retains its interest throughout the year. The grassy leaves are arranged on narrow 30cm (1ft) panicles.

The plant needs good loamy potting compost: either a mixture made up from equal parts by bulk of loam, leafmould and sand or John Innes No. 1 Potting Compost. It needs plenty of water whilst growing, but only enough in winter to keep it just damp. Temperatures should not drop below 10c (50F) and the plant benefits from an occasional liquid feed with fertilizer during the summer months. It is propagated by division of the roots in spring.

Smilax aspera 'Maculata'

GREENBRIAR

In Edwardian days it was fashionable to drape long sprays of *Asparagus plumosus*, *A. sprengeri*, or a plant commonly called smilax, but in reality another species of asparagus (*A. asparagoides*), over the sides and along the tops of tablecloths at dinner receptions. Hostesses set much store by this practice, gardeners were instructed to grow the plants in their greenhouses, and bunches of such greenery could usually be bought in flower shops or markets. Fashions change, but small pieces are still a common accompaniment of corsage sprays, and flower arrangers value the trailing stems for mixing in floral groupings.

Like asparagus, the true smilax with 350 species is a member of the natural order Liliaceae, but unlike the true lilies the flowers are insignificant, being very small, in axillary umbels and usually greenish, whitish or yellowish in colour. These are often overlooked but when they go on to fruit the clusters of round, black or red berries are quite attractive. Smilax species are commonly known as greenbriars because of their prickly green stems.

Smilax aspera is a native of southern Europe. It is a vigorous, much-branched vine which clambers up and over other plants by means of its hooked spines and tendrils. Its leathery, evergreen leaves are variable in shape but most frequently they have a triangular heart shape, sharply pointed at the tips with five to nine stout veins. Each is approximately 4–10cm (1½–4in) long and the berries are red. The variety 'Maculata' is the more decorative with conspicuous white blotches between the veins. *S. aspera* can be grown outside in warm protected situations which receive little or no frost, or it can be kept in pots and put under cover for winter. A well-drained soil with plenty of humus and full sun are the main essentials, and plenty of water during the growing season. The plant is propagated by division of the tuberous rootstock.

The young shoots of *S. aspera* are eaten like asparagus in southern Europe and sarsaparilla is obtained from the rootstocks of several species.

Solanum marginatum

MARGINED SOLANUM

Solanums belong to the natural order Solanaceae. Some – such as the tomato, *S. lycopersicum* (now more correctly *Lycopersicum esculentum*), potatoes (*S. tuberosum*) and aubergines (*S. melongena*) – have important economic uses which have made them known all over the world. Others, like *S. crispum* and *S. wendlandii* are handsome climbers which will even flower outdoors in temperate situations such as the south of Ireland or south-west England. They are also popular for growing up conservatory and greenhouse walls. In late summer they bear heavy trusses of white, blue or mauve flowers.

Several solanums have edible fruits like the kangaroo apple of Australia (*S. aviculare*) and *S. duplosinuatum* of tropical Africa. The dried stems of bittersweet (*S. dulcamara*) are used medicinally as a sedative, the leaves of *S. mammosum* from South America to treat kidney complaints, and *S. quitoense* is grown commercially in Ecuador for its acid fruits which make a refreshing drink.

The plant depicted here, *S. marginatum* from Abyssinia, makes a good pot plant. It is an upright, spiny, branching shrub, growing to 1.2m (4ft) with 20cm (8in), oblong-ovate, sinuately-lobed leaves. These leaves are densely frosted on both sides when young, but as they age the upper surface becomes greenish-white and their margins take on a glittering line of whitish dusty pubescence. The leaves also bear prickles along the veins on both upper- and under-surfaces. The species is sometimes planted outside as a sub-tropical bedding-plant for the summer or it can be planted in a greenhouse border when it will flower very freely. The blooms are white with blue centres, each about 2.5cm (1in) across, bunched together in the leaf axils. These are followed by round, prickly, yellow fruits about 4cm (1½in) across.

S. marginatum will grow in any good soil or potting compost but benefits from monthly feeds with a liquid fertilizer during the growing season. Keep the plants only just moist in winter and in a frost-free house; temperatures should not fall below 10c (50f). Plants can be increased from seed or by careful division.

Sonerila margaritacea

[NO COMMON NAME]

This small, evergreen, half-shrubby plant belongs to the natural order Melas-tomataceae, and like most members of this family (which has about 175 species, all from tropical Asia) has its veins arranged in longitudinal fashion from the base of the leaf to its tip, instead of radiating towards the edges like the open fingers of a hand.

Sonerila margaritacea comes from Java. Its specific name, *margaritacea*, means pearly, a reference to the silvery dots which sprinkle the foliage. The oval-oblong leaves 8–10cm (3–4in) in length with slightly toothed margins are produced in great abundance on reddish stems. Later in the year numerous spikes of short-lived three-petalled rosy flowers provide an added attraction. Several cultivars are available from house-plant specialists, usually with heavier speckles or silver blotches on the foliage. 'Argentea' is a well known example.

Being of tropical origin *Sonerila margaritacea* needs plenty of warmth and humidity. Winter temperatures should not drop below 15c (60f) or the leaves will fall off. It does well in centrally-heated houses or warm green-houses, where it requires water in all seasons – although naturally this should not be applied too freely. Bright sunshine causes the leaves to shrivel, so pro-tect the plant from this hazard. In time, a well-grown plant will attain a height of 60cm (24in) and as much across.

Sonerila plants can be grown in loamless compost (see Introduction, p. x) or in a mix made up from equal parts of rough peat, broken small, and sharp sand, some chopped sphagnum moss, and a few pieces of charcoal and broken crocks.

Propagation can be effected from seed or cuttings of young growth taken in spring and rooted under glass with bottom heat.

Tussilago farfara 'Variegata'

VARIEGATED COLTSFOOT

The species *Tussilago farfara* is a native of Europe, Asia, North Africa and North America; it belongs to the natural order Compositae. It is often found growing in moist places, especially on heavy clay soil and along river banks, and takes its name from *tussus*, a cough, because the dried leaves were at one time used medicinally for colds, coughs and bronchial catarrh. The foliage is also eaten as a vegetable or used for tea, while the young leaves provide an ingredient for soups and may be smoked in herbal tobaccos to alleviate asthma.

The coltsfoot is one of the earliest-flowering plants in the wild, its small yellow dandelion-like blossoms providing bright patches of colour, particularly conspicuous since they appear before the foliage. The latter comes, after the blooms have withered, as roundish heart-shaped leaves with toothed margins, covered with cobweb pubescence above and white wool beneath. In the past this thick cottony substance, when impregnated with saltpetre, was used to provide an excellent tinder.

The variegated-leaved form looks best against a dark background where its creamy-white blotches and margins show to advantage. Occasionally odd leaves appear which are almost entirely white

However, since the long fleshy, underground rhizomatous roots spread rapidly and indiscriminately, the common coltsfoot is not a plant to establish rashly in gardens, although the variegated form is much less invasive. It is best kept to banks or wild gardens, or in special areas where the roots can be confined by planting them between panes of old glass or sheets of slate thrust vertically into the ground.

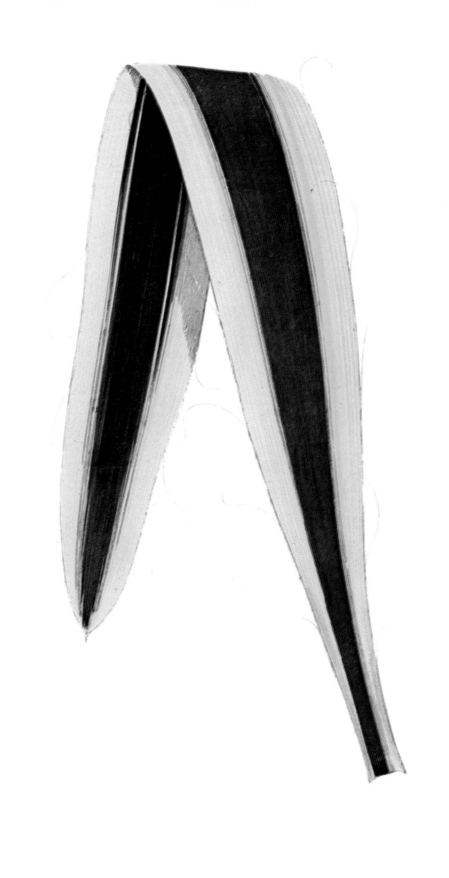

Yucca filamentosa 'Variegata'

ADAM'S NEEDLE

Yuccas are handsome evergreens belonging to the natural order Liliaceae, but with the habit of palm trees. There are about forty species, mostly from Central America, Mexico, southern United States and the West Indies, of which the variegated form of *Yucca filamentosa*, which was introduced in 1720, is a particular garden favourite. It is also one of the hardiest, given a hot, dry, well-drained position in full sun.

Yucca filamentosa is a stemless perennial with long, lanceolate, slightly glaucous foliage, arranged in a rosette. The leaves may be erect or spreading and up to 30–75cm (1–2½ft) long and 4–10cm (1½–4in) wide, with numerous curly white threads torn away from their margins. The form 'Variegata' has pale yellow leaves margined and striped with two shades of green, the edges towards the base slightly tinged with pink. The flowers appear from mid to late summer from the centres of the rosettes, borne on erect downy-stemmed panicles 1–2m (3–6ft) high. Each creamy white blossom is 5–7.5cm (2–3in) long.

Yucca flowers are pollinated by a night-flying moth, which is possibly why the blooms stand out so well in the twilight. However this moth does not exist in Europe so fertile seed is only obtained after hand-pollination. It is however possible to propagate plants from offsets – essential with the variegated kinds. The offsets appear round the side of large mature plants and make their own roots. When this occurs they may be carefully detached and planted in a shady border for a year, after which they may be transplanted to their permanent quarters.

The fibres from *Yucca filamentosa* leaves were at one time used for various textiles, such as saddle mats and sailors' hammocks, until modern materials made this unnecessary. The fruits were eaten by American Indians who also used the roots (which have saponifying properties) for washing clothes and for other forms of cleaning.

Yucca filamentosa is sometimes known as Adam's needle, or silk grass.

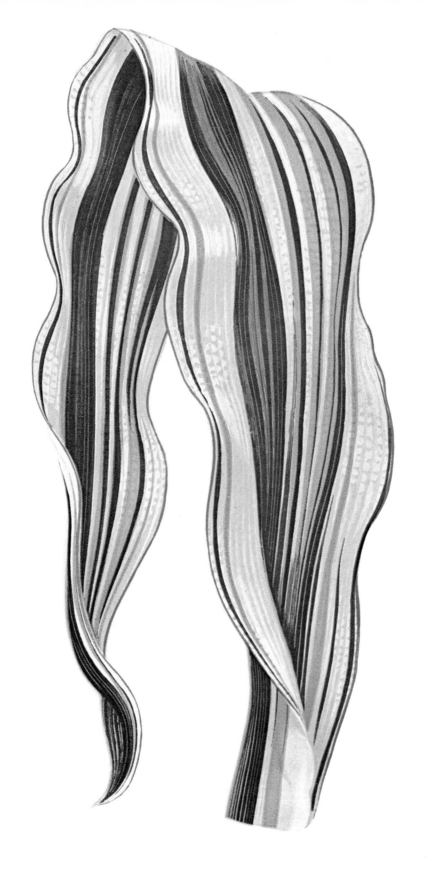

Zea mays 'Quadricolor'

ORNAMENTAL MAIZE

This giant grass is one of our most useful horticultural novelties and it is an interesting plant because of the constancy of its variegation, although it can only be multiplied by means of seed. Well worth growing in a large pot in a greenhouse or sun room it is perhaps in the open border that this fine maize displays its beauties to best advantage. It is often planted in what are commonly called sub-tropical borders or used as a 'dot' plant between smaller-growing summer-bedding plants.

The history of maize goes far back in time. Many early tribes of South American Indians grew it for food, so that countless forms developed over the years, particularly in the eastern Andes. In southern Peru primitive forms are still grown, although no wild maize as such has ever been found.

Ideally 'Quadricolor' should be started under glass in gentle heat and in individual pots of light rich soil in early spring. They then make strong plants for planting outside when all risk of frost is passed. The alternative is to sow the seed outside where it is to grow in late spring, preferably in groups 15cm (6in) apart and 10cm (4in) deep. The soil should be light and rich but well-drained, although plenty of water is necessary during the growing season. Outside sowings, however, will mature considerably later than those raised under glass. Like many variegated plants raised from seed the young plants are green at first and only acquire their rich colouring as they approach maturity. When fully developed they are 1.2m (4ft) tall and superbly marked with longitudinal bands of white and grey and sometimes a trace of rose pink. Others with striking foliage, also raised from seed, include 'Gracillima' which is 90cm (3ft) and has green and yellow variegations, and the taller 120cm (4ft) 'Harlequin', green and red striped, with deep red seeds.

A Note on Benjamin Fawcett

ENGRAVER AND PRINTER
by Ray Desmond

When the *Gardener's Chronicle* reviewed Shirley Hibberd's *New and Rare Beautiful-leaved Plants* (1870), it was ecstatic in its praise of the plates:

'First observe the tinting of the leaves, and the groundwork of such a subject as *Solanum marginatum* as a sample of the whole. Then accept the information that these pictures are not chromolithographs,* not coloured by hand, they are all, from first to last, *wood engravings;* and we imagine, but cannot of course express an opinion on the subject, that as works of art, representative of the present state of an important industry, they are not simply interesting, but remarkable.'

This perceptive appreciation of these wood engravings was far in advance of its time, for it is only now that the outstanding quality of the work of Benjamin Fawcett and his team of craftsmen is being recognised.

Benjamin Fawcett was born in December 1808 in the small Yorkshire town of Bridlington. When he was fourteen he was apprenticed to William Forth, a printer, bookseller, and stationer in the market town of Pocklington. As a young man he is reputed to have made the acquaintance of the great wood engraver Thomas Bewick, who may have instructed or at least have initiated him in the craft. About 1831 he established his own business as a bookseller, stationer, and printer in Driffield, in the East Riding of Yorkshire, and soon began publishing a series of children's copy books for which he engraved the illustrations. Over the years he sold as many as 300,000 copies of these drawing books. His business and his reputation began to flourish after he had met the Reverend Francis Orpen Morris, vicar of the nearby village of Nafferton. Their mutual interest in natural history resulted in a harmonious and profitable collaboration in a number of popular books on the subject, with Morris writing the text and Fawcett supplying the engravings. Their first joint effort, *Bible Natural History*, was published in 1849 by Richard Groombridge, who continued to employ Fawcett to illustrate many of his books.

Their reputation was firmly established with *A History of British Birds*, the first part of which appeared in June 1850. Groombridge, who cautiously

---

* Some antiquarian booksellers in their catalogues still erroneously describe the plates as chromolithographs.

had printed only a thousand copies, was surprised and delighted by its immediate success and told Morris that 'universal satisfaction is gained by this class of publication and we certainly think the field is a wide one, and an open one, and would respectfully urge you to pursue it.'

Public approval of this ambitious work in six volumes, for which Fawcett engraved 358 plates, was the turning point in his career. He moved to larger premises in a Georgian house, which he converted into printing, engraving, colouring, and binding rooms. Fawcett abandoned his retail business, having decided to concentrate upon his more profitable printing and engraving contracts. In 1852 the first numbers of *A Natural History of the Nests and Eggs of British Birds* and *A History of British Butterflies* appeared. Hand-colouring is evident on the plates of all the books so far mentioned and E. J. Lowe's *Ferns, British and Exotic* (1855–1860) was probably the first book Fawcett printed wholly in colour.

At the beginning of the nineteenth century engravers had a variety of processes at their disposal: line-engraving, etching, aquatint, mezzotint, stipple, and wood engraving. Wood engraving enjoyed a revival after Thomas Bewick had demonstrated the versatility of the medium to convey the texture of fur, feather, and foliage in his delicate vignettes for his *General History of Quadrupeds* (1790) and *History of British Birds* (1797). Bewick carved his design on the end grain of boxwood, cutting away those areas he wanted to appear white in the design. Boxwood was used because its exceptional hardness enabled him to cut very fine lines. Through his apprentices Bewick founded a new school of wood engraving, which because of its very virtuosity was to degenerate into the facsimile engravings of the mid-nineteenth century. During the 1840s coloured wood engravings began to appear. They were produced by the use of multiple woodblocks, each one printing a different colour and carefully impressed on the page.

The colour printing of George Baxter and Edmund Evans is probably far better known than the colour woodblocks of Benjamin Fawcett, yet his work is in no way inferior to theirs. His innate modesty and reluctance to leave his native Yorkshire must to some extent account for his relative obscurity. He saw no need to go outside East Driffield, which then numbered about 4,000 inhabitants, for apprentices for his establishment. He usually engaged them at an early age; his colourists, for instance, started their training at about thirteen or fourteen. According to the Reverend M. C. F. Morris, who wrote a life of Fawcett in 1925, he 'liked the girls to join his establishment about the age of fourteen or fifteen; but occasionally one could come as early as thirteen, and every one of them received most careful training.' He took a paternal interest in his staff, teaching them the rudiments of their craft, patiently supervising and correcting their work. He could have been William Morris's exemplar of the dedicated craftsman, whose enthusiasm persuaded even his wife and daughters to assist in the hand-colouring of the wood engravings.

Fawcett was a perfectionist who would not tolerate shoddy work. Conservative by nature, he stubbornly refused for many years to make use of photography for transferring drawings to the woodblocks. He usually printed from the woodblocks themselves, seldom from electrotypes (which was common practice). He obtained his paper in bulk from France and manufactured his inks from the best materials available from the London colour merchants. His personal supervision of every stage of colour production and printing ensured the impeccable standards he set himself. He imported his boxwood direct from Turkey in short logs, about five feet in length and ten inches in diameter, which were then sawn into slabs one inch in thickness and stacked in racks to mature for at least three years before they were cut up for engraving blocks.

W. D. Ridley, one of Fawcett's best engravers, suggested one paramount reason for the success of his firm:

'It was a community, a *family* almost of men, women and girls, every one of them trained from entrance to do their particular work. . . . If there was a secret which produced the fine results it has just been indicated. The whole staff worked together, proudly trying to get the best results. The finest plates were printed on hand presses, and the London reviewers occasionally "came a cropper", when they described the plates as very fine examples of "Chromolitho". It is easy to see the reason for their mistake, for in the first place the working of the key blocks, and also the colour blocks, consisted of such fine lines as to make it almost impossible for any one to detect the method; and this, added to the fact that the blocks themselves were used – never an electro in any case – accounts for the peculiar grain which is so characteristic of the Driffield work; for coloured inks leave the surface of end grain boxwood and other woods with some reluctance, so to speak; and the result is that in most cases, in distant views of mountains, landscape backgrounds, and such like, the colours are to some extent transparent and luminous, thus giving just that charm of atmosphere and distance, and the water-colour effect spoken of above.'

Fawcett's rich colours enhance the pages of many Victorian books, especially those published by Richard Groombridge, a successful populariser of natural-history literature. One of Groombridge's most prolific authors was Shirley Hibberd, a horticultural journalist and editor whose fluent pen produced a flow of modestly priced manuals such as *Garden Favourites* (1858), *The Fern Garden* (1869), *Field Flowers* (1870), *The Amateur's Flower Garden* (1871), *The Amateur's Greenhouse* (1873), *The Amateur's Rose Garden* (1874), and *The Amateur's Kitchen Garden* (1877), all with Fawcett plates, many of which had already appeared in *The Floral World*, a magazine edited by Hibberd for Groombridge. Hibberd's *Rustic Adornments for Homes of Taste* (1856) has some of Fawcett's earliest fully printed colour plates. This charming specimen of the Victorian gift book was followed by *The Ivy* (1872), with Fawcett colour blocks of a pastel softness. *The Ivy*, which reflected a Victorian fashion for variegated-leaved plants, was a successor to Hibberd's best work, *New and Rare Beautiful-leaved Plants* (1870). The colours of all the fifty-four plates done by Fawcett for this book are in perfect register, no easy achievement.

Nine years earlier, Edward Joseph Lowe had completed a similar work, *Beautiful Leaved Plants* (1861). Lowe, a man of independent means and a Fellow of the Royal Society, spent his days happily engaged in scientific research at his home at Shirenewton in Gwent. His *Ferns, British and Exotic* (1855–60) was based largely on his superb fern collection. The *Gardener's Chronicle* complained that some of the plates, executed by Fawcett's firm, 'fail to give any tolerable idea of the plants they profess to represent.' Fawcett's engravers fell below their normal high standards in their clumsy rendering of the fine grass spikelets in Lowe's *Natural History of British Grasses* (1858). They redeemed themselves, however, with *Beautiful Leaved Plants*, which the book designer Ruari McLean has judged to be 'a triumph of wood-engraving and colour printing.' It was issued in twenty parts at a shilling each between 1859 and 1861. Some traces of hand-colouring can be detected on a few of its sixty colour woodblocks. Its success merited the reprints brought out by Groombridge in 1864, 1865, and 1868, and another publisher reissued it in 1872 and 1891. A French edition, translated by J. Rothschild, was published in Paris in 1865: *Les plantes à feuillage coloré, recueil des espèces les plus remarquables servant à la décoration des jardins, des serres et des appartements*. According to *The Bookseller* (7 March 1893), it was selected as a worthy example of high-class printing at the Paris Exhibition for presentation to the Empress Eugénie. It was reissued in Paris from 1867 to 1870 in two volumes, the second volume containing fifty-two coloured plates from Shirley Hibberd's *New and Rare Beautiful-leaved Plants*, which had been published in eighteen one-shilling parts during 1868 and 1869 before being issued in book form in 1870.

The artist who drew the plates for these two books was Alexander Francis Lydon (1836–1917), who, with his younger brother Frederick, had been apprenticed to Fawcett to learn wood engraving. His facility with pencil and brush was soon discovered and he became Fawcett's resident artist. Amazingly industrious, he executed more than 1,500 drawings before he left the firm in 1883. Some of his best work appears in F. O. Morris's *County Seats* (*c.* 1864–80) and W. Houghton's *British Fresh-water Fishes* (1879).

Benjamin Fawcett died in 1893. Although much of the later work produced by his firm came from the hands of his engravers and his artist Lydon, it is true to say that they were all impressed by his dedication to his craft, inspired by his high standards, and encouraged by his constant concern for his staff.

Glossary

ALTERNATE used to denote an arrangement of leaves, one rising above another on the opposite side of the stem.

ANTHER the part of the stamen that contains the pollen.

APEX used of the tip of a shoot.

AROID (from Latin *arum*) a plant with a large spathe, enclosing a fleshy spadix, belonging to the genus *Araceae*.

AXIL the angle between a leaf and the stem from which it rises.

BIPINNATE used to describe segmented leaves that are further subdivided, i.e., twice pinnate (see plate 52).

BRACT a small leaf-like growth, sometimes brightly coloured, usually at the base of a flower or flower cluster.

BROMELIAD used of the natural order Bromeliaceae, to which the pineapple belongs.

CALYX, CALYCES the leaves or sepals providing the outer whorl of the perianth, or bud covering.

CAUDEX the trunk or stem, i.e., central axis, of a fern or palm.

CLONE group of identical plants produced by vegetative (i.e., not by seed) propagation from one parent plant.

CORDATE describes a heart-shaped leaf (see plates 44 & 57).

CRENATE describes a leaf with round-toothed edges (see plates 12 & 20).

CULTIVAR a cultivated variety of plant, as opposed to a naturally occurring variety.

CYME an inflorescence with a single terminal flower and lateral side branches.

DENTATE describes a sharp-toothed leaf (see plates 2 & 27).

EPIPHYTE a plant that lives above the soil drawing nourishment either from the air (as do some orchids) or from debris lodged in a tree trunk, branch, or rock.

FIMBRIATE describes a leaf or flower with fringed edges.

FLORET one of the little flowers that make up a large head or cluster.

FROND a technical term for a fern.

GENUS, GENERA see introduction, page xiv.

GLAUCOUS refers to leaves covered with 'bloom', a grey-green or white patina.

HUMUS compost, well-decayed vegetable matter, in the form of a brown, crumbly, sweet-smelling material.

LANCEOLATE describes a long, thin leaf (see plate 21).

LOAM used in this book to mean good-quality soil, containing clay, sand, silt, humus, and minerals. It holds moisture but it should be neither wet nor dry and sandy.

MONOECIOUS having individual male and female flowers on the same plant.

MONOTYPIC a genus containing only one species.

NODE a point or joint on a stem from which leaves or side shoots arise.

OPPOSITE applying to leaves arranged in pairs on opposite sides of the stem.

OFFSETS a short sideways offshoot from a root or stem.

OSMUNDA flowering fern, *Osmunda regalis*.

OVATE describes a leaf with an egg-shaped outline (see plates 10 & 34).

PALMATE describes a leaf shaped like the palm of a hand (see plates 1 & 3).

PANICLE a loose, branching cluster of flowers.

PEAT common moss peat is organic matter deriving from sphagnum, and sedge peat from sedges and similar plants. They both provide humus.

PETAL each of the divisions of the corolla of a flower.

PINNATE describes a compound leaf having leaflets arranged on either side of a stalk, like a feather (see plate 45).

PUBESCENT describes a leaf covered with soft down (see plate 62).

RHIZOME root-like stem growing horizontally underground.

SAGITTATE describes a leaf shaped like an arrow (see plate 19).

SAPOGENIN a crystalline compound derived from many plants.

SCION a shoot, twig, or bud separated from one plant to join another (by budding or grafting).

SEPAL a division of the calyx of a flower.

SEQUESTRENE also known as iron chelates. A substance applied to certain plants to remedy an iron deficiency.

SINUATE describes a leaf with a sinuous, wavy edge (see plate 64).

SPADIX a form of flower consisting of a thick, fleshy spike with small flowers enclosed in a spathe. See Aroid.

SPATHE a large bract or leaf enclosing and protecting the spadix of aroids.

SPHAGNUM a type of moss found in bogs and swamps.

SPIKE a narrow form of inflorescence consisting of stalkless flowers arranged close to a central stem.

STAMEN the male reproductive organ of a plant.

STOLON a stem that creeps across the soil, rooting at the tip or nodes.

TRUSS a compact flower cluster on a stalk.

TUBER a thickened stem, usually underground, that provides a storage organ and points for new growth.

UMBEL describes an arrangement in which all the individual flower stalks rise from the one point.

ZONAL describes leaves marked with zones of colour, as, e.g., pelargonium.

Index of plants